Integrity at Work

Integrity at Work

Finding Your Ethical Compass
in a Post-Enron World

NORMAN L. GEISLER
AND RANDY DOUGLASS

BakerBooks

Grand Rapids, Michigan

Published by Baker Books
a division of Baker Publishing Group
P.O. Box 6287, Grand Rapids, MI 49516-6287
www.bakerbooks.com

Printed in the United States of America

Library of Congress Cataloging-in-Publication Data
Geisler, Norman L.
    Integrity at work : finding your ethical compass in a post-Enron world / Norman L. Geisler and Randy Douglass.
        p.   cm.
    Includes bibliographical references.
    ISBN 10: 0-8010-6771-5 (pbk.)
    ISBN 978-0-8010-6771-6 (pbk.)
    1. Work—Moral and ethical aspects. 2. Business ethics. 3. Employees—Conduct of life.
4. Work—Religious aspects—Christianity. I. Douglass, Randy. II. Title.
HD4905.G44 2007
174′.4—dc22   2006100558

Contents

Acknowledgments

We would like to thank the staff at Baker Books for believing in the vision of this book. People like Robert Hosack, Cheryl Van Andel, Karen Steele, Rachel Geerlings, and Paul Brinkerhoff, our project editor, made writing this book a pleasure.

Special thanks go to Christina Woodside and Lanny Wilson for their invaluable expertise in coordinating the communicational logistics of two authors in two different cities. Their professionalism, administrative skill, editorial ability, and encouraging spirit make them rare gems indeed.

This book is a reality because of our wives, Barbara Geisler and Kristie Douglass, who have been our constant source of support and encouragement in the need for and the writing process of this book.

Finally, this book is dedicated to those who desire to exemplify Micah 6:8 in the workplace. May their tribe increase!

> He has showed you, O man, what is good.
>   And what does the LORD require of you?
> To act justly and to love mercy
>   and to walk humbly with your God.

Introduction

Most companies have policies and memos governing the way they are to do business. Consider a portion of this company's *2000 Code of Ethics* under a section titled "Business Ethics":

> Employees of _____ are charged with conducting their business affairs in accordance with the highest ethical standards. An employee shall not conduct himself or herself in a manner which directly or indirectly would be detrimental to the best interests of the Company or in a manner which would bring to the employee financial gain separately derived as a direct consequence of his or her employment with the Company. Moral as well as legal obligations will be fulfilled openly, promptly, and in a manner which will reflect pride on the Company's name. . . . Advertising and promotion will be truthful, not exaggerated or misleading. Agreements, whether contractual or verbal, will be honored. No bribes, bonuses, kickbacks, lavish entertainment, or gifts will be given or received in exchange for special position, price or privilege.[1]

This is but a small section of this company's code of ethics; all in all, it appears to be pretty good. Statements such as "highest ethical standards," "moral as well as legal obligations," and "no bribes, bonuses, kickbacks" seem to cover all the bases in ethical behavior.

Except for one thing: apparently, no one read the memo. You see, this is the *2000 Code of Ethics* for the Enron Corporation. Yes, Enron had a code of ethics. Not only that, the code of ethics began with a memo from Ken Lay in which he said, "As officers and employees of Enron Corp . . . we are responsible for conducting the business affairs of the Company in accordance with all applicable laws and in a moral and honest manner."[2] To top it off, everyone who worked for the company had to sign a compliance statement. Think of what

9

would have happened if Enron's leadership had actually followed their own code of ethics.

Today, Enron has become synonymous with corporate greed and corruption. In fact, *BusinessWeek Online* reports that the 2003 *Webster's New World Finance and Investment Dictionary* defines "Enronitus" as the "nervousness over a company because of suspected accounting problems."[3]

Clearly a better ethical compass is needed in the moral morass of today's marketplace. Hopefully the following pages will help fill this void. One thing appears certain: if we do not live by what is beyond us, then what is within us will be dragged down by what is below us. Business desperately needs an ethical compass.

The Ethical Morass of Today's Workplace

1

Marketplace Ethics—Lost in a Wilderness

The Corporate World Is Lost

Today's corporate world is lost in work's ethical wilderness. What did Enron, WorldCom, Adelphia, Global Crossing, ImClone, and Martha Stewart bring to mind when they were in the news? The desperate need for integrity!

Business executives did not fare very well in the Gallup Organization's 2004 "Honesty and Ethics Poll," which surveyed the public's perception of professional morality. For example, of twenty-one professions, North Americans identified nurses as most honest, but business executives ranked seventeenth, ahead of congressmen, lawyers, advertising practitioners, and finally, car salespeople.[1]

A March 2005 Gallup poll showed that 59 percent of Americans surveyed were "somewhat dissatisfied" (29 percent) or "very dissatisfied" (30 percent) with the United States' moral and ethical climate.[2] A May 2005 Gallup poll on confidence in institutions ranked public confidence in big business fourteenth out of fifteen, just in front of HMOs![3] This is sad when one realizes that 90 percent of business schools now provide some form of training in business ethics.[4]

Don't expect the corporate world to find its ethical way anytime soon. In October, the Josephson Institute of Ethics—a nonprofit organization that conducts training in business ethics and character education—released their 2006 Josephson Institute Report Card. The Institute surveyed 36,122 U.S. high school students and found that on a personal level:

- 98% believe good character is important
- 94% believe trust and honesty are essential in business and the workplace
- 89% believe goodness is more important than wealth

However, when it came to what their perception was of what works in the real world:

- 59% believe that to be successful, you do what you have to do, even cheat
- 42% believe a person has to lie or cheat to succeed
- 23% or more than one in five believe that people willing to lie, cheat or steal are more likely to be successful

In reference to their own personal conduct:

- 60% have cheated on an exam in the past year
- 28% have stolen from a store
- 39% have lied to save money[5]

If you think these teens won't cheat or steal when they enter the workforce, you're only kidding yourself.

The workplace can be seen as an ethical wilderness filled with mazes, bogs, and steep cliffs. Employers have the difficult task of leading their employees through this ethical wilderness. They have asked us the following questions:

- How do we hire the right people and fire the wrong, all the while staying out of the courtroom?
- How do we compensate well enough to keep good employees while at the same time not decreasing necessary profit?
- Do we provide a safe environment for our employees?
- How can we afford the health-care costs that employees expect us to cover?
- Is it possible to be a leader who is both fair and firm?
- How does one develop and keep the proper balance between profit and people?

To look at the last question first, an article in *Leadership Advantage* states that the balance between profit and people is a proper balance of the ends and means.

An analysis of the relationship between ethical behavior and effective leadership reveals that it is a matter of choosing both the ends and the means. A business enterprise must be profitable in order to survive. Service organizations must satisfy consumers' expectations. Government must meet the needs of its citizens. The ends are the very reason for existence of the enterprise.

At the same time, the means by which they achieve those ends are increasingly important. Placing value on short term gains at the detriment of long term results ends in disaster. The demise of a company is a tragedy because it affects the lives of families. Families depend on the responsible decisions of business leaders. At the core of all business decisions are moral and ethical principles. Failure to support and withhold high standards has consequences.[6]

How can one obtain and maintain this balance when dealing with the competing demands of business and people? Even this article struggles to come up with a clear and workable answer.

Employees face the difficult task of being led through the ethical wilderness of work and have asked us the following questions:

- How do I develop a work ethic that includes a healthy view of success?
- How should I respond when co-workers steal supplies or time from the company?
- How do I keep the proper balance between work and home?
- How can I get along with co-workers who act more like animals than people?
- How do I obey policies with which I don't agree?
- How can I respect my boss when he or she is not worthy of it?

Those charged with the overall management of companies face the ethical wilderness of dealing with customers. We have heard these questions from them:

- How do we sell our product in an honest way?
- What do we do if our product is not of the best quality?
- How do we set a fair price for providing our goods?
- How do we maintain customer service without ending up in customer servitude?
- How do we handle customer complaints in a way that is fair to both the customer and the company?

Marketplace Responses to the Ethical Wilderness

How does the marketplace respond to its ethical dilemmas? John Maxwell lists three ways.[7]

1. Teach Remedial Ethics

When students struggle in a class, often the school will send them to a remedial class where they relearn the basics. Maxwell quotes Joan Ryan, columnist for the *San Francisco Chronicle*, when he writes that businesses are now doing the same thing. Corporations are contracting with "ethics" consulting firms and hiring ethics officers. "These officers produce and distribute thick manuals that often read like tax codes, complete with loopholes and fine print."[8] Ryan warns her readers not to be impressed by this new heart of the business world for ethics. She says, "This isn't about being ethical. It's about evading punishment. Under federal guidelines, companies that have ethics programs are eligible for reduced fines if convicted of wrong-doing."[9]

2. Perform an Ethics Flea Dip

A second approach is to reeducate ethical offenders to improve their actions for the future. Management consultant Frank J. Navran calls this approach an "ethical flea dip."[10] It is like giving a dog a flea dip in the summer to get rid of fleas and ticks. More fleas and ticks are always waiting in the grass, and sure enough, they'll find their way to the dog. If the company's environment encourages unethical behavior, the flea dip will not work, and the bugs will soon return.

3. Rely on the Law

Some companies let the government set ethical standards and look only at what is technically legal for their decision making. Scary thought, right?

In his "Complete Guide to Ethics Management: Ethics Toolkit for Managers," Carter McNamara gives "10 Myths about Business Ethics." Myth 9 is "Our organization is not in trouble with the law, so we're ethical." He writes:

> One can often be unethical, yet operate within the limits of the law, e.g., withhold information from superiors, fudge on budgets, constantly complain about others, etc. However, breaking the law often starts with unethical behavior that has gone unnoticed. The "boil the frog" phenomena is a useful parable here: If you put a frog in hot water, it immediately jumps out. If you put a frog in cool water and slowly heat up the water, you can eventually boil the frog. The frog doesn't seem to notice the adverse change in its environment.[11]

The corporate world today is lost in an ethical wilderness, and they know it.

The Christian World Is Lost

In an article on being a Christian in the workplace, *Fortune Small Business* senior editor Richard McGill Murphy writes:

Christian entrepreneurs are more likely to see their offices and factories as extensions of their beliefs. They strive to accommodate evangelism to an evolving body of workplace law based on the separation of church and state. And on a more personal level, many struggle to reconcile the often hard-edged requirements of commerce with the teachings of Christ. . . . They ask themselves: Is it right to lay off workers to boost profits, or only to save the company? How do you foster a Christian office culture without violating the rights of non-Christian employees? What if you can't get a city contract without bending the law?[12]

For those in the workplace, the struggle to maintain good ethics is faced every day. How well is the struggle being handled? Is the Christian world lost as well in work's ethical wilderness?

You be the judge. A survey was distributed to 300 Christian men and women in business on the ethical dimensions of their jobs. Some disturbing responses are quoted at the end of this chapter. But now let's look more generally at the survey results:

1. *How would they rate their company ethically?* A mere 16 percent described their company as "very ethical," but 58 percent rated their company as "somewhat ethical," in that it makes decisions based on good ethical standards *some* of the time. One can only wonder what causes lapses in standards to occur. Twenty-six percent said that their company is not ethical at all. One person admitted that his company's unwritten motto is "What can we get away with?"

2. *How often do these Christians face ethical decisions and dilemmas at work?*

   • Daily—74%
   • Weekly—16%
   • Monthly—5%
   • Hardly at all—5%

3. *List the ethical decisions or dilemmas you face at work.* If you doubt the description of work as an ethical wilderness, reflect on the types of issues Christians are facing:

   • Good attitude at work—77%
   • Difficult co-workers—74%
   • Difficult customers—66%
   • Laziness or low motivation at work—65%
   • Disagreeing with the boss properly—58%
   • Supporting the boss and/or company—51%
   • Sexual pressures—44%
   • Balance of work and family—42%
   • Dishonesty—40%

- Refraining from witnessing—32%
- Hiring employees properly—30%
- Cheating others—30%
- Firing employees properly—28%
- Keeping your word—26%
- Profit—14%
- Stealing from the company—8%

4. *How well did you handle these ethical issues?* The answers are alarming. While 26 percent answered that they felt they handle ethical issues well, 74 percent said that they do not. Remember that these are Christians who face ethical issues at work every day, and 74 percent do not handle them well.

5. *When facing ethical decisions, where do you turn for help?* We can see the reason 74 percent of these Christians handled ethical issues poorly when we examine their sources of counsel.

   - Only 10 percent go to their pastor for advice. While they respect their pastor for advice on the spiritual world, they recognize that many pastors have little, if any, experience in the business world and thus can provide little comfort and guidance. When a pastor was asked if he addressed business issues from the pulpit, he stated, "No. I've been in the church for thirty-five years. It is the only world that I know."
   - Thirty-six percent turn to the Bible for advice on business affairs. That low percentage is not surprising, for many Christians know very little about what the Bible has to say about the business world. This book will reveal a wealth of wisdom on business ethics that the Bible offers.
   - Seventy-one percent said that they turn to God for help. Since they are not turning to the Bible, this must mean they are turning to prayer when in trouble. We all know that praying in times of trouble often does not go beyond "Help me out of this mess, Lord!" We need to pray as we study the Scriptures, asking God to reveal his wisdom to us (James 1:5).
   - Forty-eight percent said that they turn to a co-worker or friend for advice. Counsel is good (Prov. 15:22), but one needs to make sure it is godly counsel (Ps. 1:1–2).
   - Six percent said they turn to a business book for advice on ethics. That is troubling if, as we have seen, the corporate world and much of the Christian business world are lost in work's ethical wilderness. Good Christian books on business ethics are rare.

6. *Would you be interested in a book to show you how to make ethical decisions at work?* Ninety-seven percent said they would be interested in such a

book. That is why this book was written. Even Christians are lost in the ethical wilderness of work and need something to guide them.

A Compass Is Needed

Almost anywhere you are on Earth, you can hold a compass in your hand and it will always point toward the earth's magnetic North Pole. Imagine that it is a cloudy day and you are stranded on a boat in the middle of the ocean. As you look in every direction, all you can see is water. How in the world can you know which direction to go without a compass? Now imagine that you are in a thick forest in the Smoky Mountains on a cloudy day and have lost your way. What do you do? Long before GPS satellites and other high-tech navigational aids, if you were lost, the compass was the easiest and surest way to find your way home.

A compass is needed to guide us in the ethical wilderness of work as well. Consider the following reasons. First, without a compass we are lost. We have seen that the business world, both corporate and Christian, is lost in an ethical wilderness. We need help to find our way out. Maxwell says, "Where once our decisions were based on ethics, now ethics are based on our decisions."[13] We seem to stick a finger in the air to find out which way the wind is blowing and then go that way. Politicians today tend to be governed more by polls than principles. People follow the crowd just to see where they are going.

Second, a compass has a fixed point—north is always north and south is always south. Only when there are fixed points is the path sure. The absolutes God gives through his Word are more fixed than magnetic north. We must find these norms when we have lost our way.

Third, a compass is a directional tool to show us the right way. If you are lost and you know that home is northwest, make sure the compass is facing toward the north, find the direction that goes northwest and then walk that path. Some who are expert at traversing a natural wilderness recommend checking the compass every one hundred yards. One who does that will never get disoriented. To find our ethical home, we must have a compass.

Even the corporate world recognizes the need for such a compass. McNamara writes:

> Values are no longer followed. Consequently, there is no clear moral compass to guide leaders through complex dilemmas about what is right or wrong. Attention to ethics in the workplace sensitizes leaders and staff to how they should act. Perhaps most important, attention to ethics in the workplace helps ensure that when leaders and managers are struggling in times of crises and confusion, they retain a strong moral compass.[14]

Conclusion

If there are ethical absolutes, how have we lost our way? We once were a society where a handshake and a man's word were his bond. But no more. We not only make unethical decisions in business but in all of life. The business world is simply a reflection of the core of the businessperson.

To understand that, we must understand how people determine what is right. That is the subject of the next chapter.

Ethics in the Workplace Questionnaire

1. I would rate my company as:
   - Very ethical (we make the right ethical decisions most of the time) —16%
   - Somewhat ethical (we make the right ethical decisions some of the time)—58%
   - Not ethical (we make the right ethical decisions hardly at all)—26%

2. I face ethical dilemmas and decisions at work:
   - Daily—74%
   - Weekly—16%
   - Monthly—5%
   - Hardly at all—4%

3. Which ethical decision or dilemma have you encountered while at work?
   - Sexual pressures—44%
   - Hiring employees properly—30%
   - Dishonesty—40%
   - Laziness—65%
   - Supporting my boss/company—51%
   - Stealing from the company—8%
   - Having a good attitude—77%
   - Difficult co-workers—74%
   - Refraining from witnessing—32%
   - Firing employees properly—28%
   - Keeping your word—26%
   - Cheating others—30%
   - Disagreeing with boss properly—58%
   - Making a profit—14%
   - Difficult customers—66%
   - Balance of family and work—42%

4. Do you feel that you handled these issues well?
   - Yes—26%
   - No—74%

5. Where do you normally turn for help when facing difficult ethical workplace decisions?
   - Pastor—10%
   - Bible—36%
   - God—71%
   - Co-worker or friend—48%
   - Business book on the subject—6%

6. Would you be interested in a book that will guide Christians in the workplace to make ethical decisions?
   - Yes—97%
   - No—3%

2

How Did We Lose Our Way?

Lost at Sea

On Sunday, April 24, 2005, Troy Driscoll, fifteen, and Josh Hunt, seventeen, go shark fishing off the Charleston, South Carolina, coast in their fourteen-foot Sunfish sailboat. They don't plan to be out long; they only want to test run the boat they have been fixing up. They leave without rudder, mast, sail, food, fresh water, or cell phone. They also ignore the small-craft advisory then in effect, with the tide going out and the wind gusting to twenty-eight knots.

They launch on an outgoing tide, and almost immediately a riptide seizes the boat. They paddle furiously, but the current is too strong. They drop anchor, but it follows behind like a fishing lure. Josh ties a rope around his chest and tries to swim to shore, but to no avail. Exhausted, he climbs back into the boat, and they watch helplessly as the shoreline shrinks in the distance. They float aimlessly like driftwood and are given up for dead by all but their family.

Amazingly, on Saturday, April 30, after seven long days, they are found by a fishing boat seven miles off Cape Fear, North Carolina, 111 miles from Charleston—alive.[1]

What led to Troy and Josh's desperate ordeal at sea leads to our desperate ordeal in the workplace: the boys left the shore without any preparation, in terrible weather conditions, and with no way to battle the current to get home. Every week we enter the tumultuous ethical sea called the workplace without any preparation for what we might face, in stormy conditions, and with no means to battle the current that pulls us away from the shore. Then we wonder how we got so far from home.

Why Do We Make Unethical Decisions?

People make unethical decisions for a number of reasons.

Relinquish

The January 18, 2002, issue of *Time* magazine featured Enron whistleblower Sharon Watkins as "Person of the Week." Watkins was Enron's vice president for corporate development at the time. In August of 2001, she wrote her boss, Ken Lay, a stinging, seven-page "pull-no-punches, put-it-on-record letter," addressing abuses of the company and the potential and probable downfall of Enron if nothing was done. It was written in such a way that showed she knew that she wasn't telling him anything he didn't already know.[2] Sharon Watkins was not about to *relinquish* her ethics and her reputation without challenging her boss, even though it could mean possible retaliation.

When confronted with a difficult choice relating to ethical principle or practice, we can choose to do what is most convenient. We can go with the flow, take the easy way out, and try not to make waves. When we "go with the flow," the current takes us into dangerous waters. Our story may not come out as well as for the two teens from Charleston.

Résumé

When confronted with a difficult choice relating to ethical principle or practice, we can choose to do what we must to get ahead. This may mean that we are the ones making the unethical decisions to further our career. We believe the old adage "Nice guys finish last."

Bill is a salesman for a company that sells powerboats. A couple comes in looking at boats, and the husband falls in love with a twenty-four-foot Stingray Powerboat 240 LS. Bill is excited. It has been a slow month. He really needs this sale to pay his mounting bills. His boss is constantly pointing out his lack of performance and talking about a change. However, as Bill goes through the financial paperwork with the couple, he realizes that this purchase will overburden the couple financially. A less expensive model will fit their needs, though it will mean less money for him.

He thinks about it for a couple of seconds before pushing through the sale. Bill chooses to further his career rather than his ethical integrity.

The résumé approach may mean that when we see our company drifting into "murky" ethical waters, we decide to do what is best for our professional future and be quiet rather than to do what is best for our spiritual future. But to keep quiet or go along with an unethical decision or action is like taking a step into quicksand: we will only keep sinking deeper.

Rewards

When confronted with a difficult choice relating to ethical principle or practice, we can choose to do what we can to gain money and pleasure. Closely related to the *résumé* concept, this approach is more concerned with the "things" a job provides than with the career itself.

A salesman for a pharmaceutical company, Tom was pressured to promote certain drugs, even after reports began to surface questioning their safety. "If I take a moral stand at work, I could lose my job, my SUV, my home with a pool, as well as my nice expense account," he said.

He was more concerned about losing toys and possessions than about losing his integrity.

Rationalize

In 2002, a period called by some the "summer of ethical despair," 84 percent of college students surveyed said they believed that the United States was experiencing a business crisis, and 77 percent believed that CEOs should be held responsible for it.

But 59 percent of the same students admitted to cheating on a test, and only 19 percent said they would report a classmate who cheated.[3] It is interesting how we can demand integrity from others while not demanding it of ourselves.

When confronted with a difficult choice relating to ethical principle or practice, we can choose to rationalize our choices. We can reason that "everyone is doing it," or we can choose according to what seems right for the moment. We may think that the work environment is a dog-eat-dog world and we have to be a dog to run with the dogs. The authors know businessmen and businesswomen who actually see a dichotomy between the world of work and the world of the church. On Sunday they think and act one way, but on Monday through Friday they think and act just like the world.

A church elder board met to determine what to do with an assistant pastor because of immorality. The senior pastor stated this was a church discipline issue and shared the biblical steps that should be taken. One elder spoke up: "I disagree. This is more of a business issue than a church issue. This pastor has a large following in the church, and if we practice discipline on him, it will lead to a loss of people and income. The business approach is to buy out his contract in a hush-hush way. Send him packing, and no one is the wiser." Many of the other elders nodded in agreement.

In ethical dilemmas, we can choose the approach of relinquishing, building the résumé, gathering rewards, or rationalizing. If we choose to protect our career instead of standing against unethical practices, sooner or later this decision will backfire. The Bible warns of such consequences. Song of Songs 2:15 says, "Catch for us the foxes, the little foxes that ruin the vineyards, our vineyards that are in bloom."

The "little foxes" are the little things—the little sins, excuses, and allowances—that we let into our lives. Such things eat away at the sweet grapes of our lives. Lie to make one sale, and it is easier to lie to make another. First Corinthians 5:6–7 warns that just a little old yeast will ruin the whole batch of dough.

Ecclesiastes 10:1 says, "As dead flies give perfume a bad smell, so a little folly outweighs wisdom and honor." This is what Watkins feared. "I am incredibly nervous that we will implode in a wave of accounting scandals," she wrote to Lay. "My eight years of Enron work history will be worth nothing on my résumé, the business world will consider the past successes as nothing but an elaborate accounting hoax."[4] She warned that Lay must do the right thing so that this "little folly" at Enron would not destroy her eight years of wisdom and honor.

He did not do the right thing. Can we do better?

Defining What Is Right

There are various views on how to make the right decision.[5]

Might Is Right

What is right is defined by whoever has the most power. This position fails to distinguish between power and goodness. This is seen in the workplace when company "demigods" lift a finger, and everyone shudders. The decisions of a rich few who wanted to get richer led to the failure of Enron, leaving four thousand people without jobs and wiping out savings and pensions. Enron went bust owing creditors sixty-five billion dollars.

Majority Is Right

What is morally right is determined by the group to which one belongs. But just because the majority rules does not mean the majority is right. Whole communities, such as Jonestown, for instance, have committed suicide. Just because the board of directors decides on a course of action does not make it the right action. The decision may benefit them but hurt many others. Just because the majority of a factory's union votes to ratify a questionable contract does not mean it is right.

Man Is Right

The right thing to do is what I decide is right. This theory implies that any act can be right, even if its intended outcome is cruel, hateful, or tyrannical. Owners of small businesses can have this attitude as they hold the fate of their employees in their hands. Many employees in small businesses are "at will," meaning they stay only as long as the owner so wills. They have no contract and thus serve at the owner's pleasure. An owner can fire employees, decimating their lives, without consequences. They have few avenues of recourse.

Moderation Is Right

Morality is found in a moderate course of action. The middle road is not always the best or ethical way of action. In fact, on the superhighway of life, being in the middle of the road is a dangerous place to be! Someone has said that compromise, which often takes one to the middle of the road, is the "oil" of business and politics. The successful CEO of a large marketing firm told one of the authors, "You have to give a little to get a little. You look the other way to get what you want. . . . It's simply the price of business." Compromise denotes a yielding of position that may have disastrous consequences. As we have already seen, going with the flow to do what is easiest and most convenient leads to being lost at sea.

Pleasure Is Right

What brings the most pleasure and least pain is right. But not all pleasures are good, and not all pain is bad. There is one company for which the bottom-line evaluatory tool for all decisions is the question, "How does this make you feel?" The premise behind this concept is that every staff member must feel good about a decision or he or she will not support and properly implement it. The staff meets to discuss a possible course of action, and each member is asked this "feeling" question. If anyone does not feel good about a potential decision, the course of action is rejected or tabled.

On the surface, this may seem wise and is especially attractive to the younger generation. But the hard reality is that many decisions are hard and do not make us "feel" good, but are nevertheless necessary. The authors have never felt good about demoting or firing an employee, but on occasion it was the right and necessary thing to do. Not only is the feel-good approach a poor way to do business; it is a narcissistic approach to life.

God's Way Is Right

The moral law comes from a moral lawgiver. Hence, whatever action God specifies as good *is good* because he is morally good by nature. Whatever action God specifies as a good action is a good action. Conversely, if God specifies an action to be evil, then it is evil. Thus, moral good is both ultimate and specifiable. This approach forms the basis for the Christian ethic. So we must know what God has to say about our course of action and respond accordingly.

The question always comes up as to the credibility of using the Bible or turning to God for guidance in business. As mentioned in chapter 1, many

Christians do not know of the wealth of business knowledge the Bible provides. Consider the following:[6]

- One hundred twenty-two of Jesus's 132 public appearances were in the workplace.
- Forty-five of Jesus's fifty-two recorded parables had a workplace context.
- In Acts, thirty-nine of the forty divine interventions were in the marketplace.
- Jesus spent more than half of his adult life as a carpenter. He worked until age thirty and only then embarked on a brief three-and-a-half year preaching ministry.
- The church was founded by businesspeople. None of the apostles or church leaders belonged to the religious establishment. Peter, Andrew, John, and James were fishermen, working in the food industry. Matthew was a tax collector and government employee. Nathanael was probably a farmer. Mark was likely a businessman. Paul constructed temporary housing. Luke was a medical doctor. The Seven (see Acts 6) all were businessmen. The first Ethiopian convert was a banker and governmental official. Dorcas (Acts 9) was a garment manufacturer, while Lydia (Acts 16) was a distributor of upscale fabrics. Cornelius was a senior military officer, and Simon the tanner had a leather goods business.
- The Gospels were written by businessmen and religious outsiders: a medical doctor, a retired tax officer, a fisherman, and Mark, who came from a wealthy family and probably ran the family business.
- The church is seen in a business setting (Acts 1, 10). It wasn't conceived in a religious setting, as in the temple or a synagogue, but in a private home—most likely owned by a businessman. For the upper room to seat at least 120, it had to be a part of a large house (1:13–15). Most houses this size had the business downstairs and the dwelling upstairs. If this is the case for this room, the church was born in a secular setting, the marketplace.
- When the moment came to introduce a revolutionary principle—that Gentiles could and should be accepted into the church—God used three marketplace leaders: Peter, Simon the tanner, and Cornelius the military officer (Acts 10). And God changed Peter's heart near a place of business—in a home associated with a tanning shop.
- The church's international headquarters were established in Antioch, a center of business and commerce.

The Bible discusses many aspects of business. It guides employers in how to treat their employees, employees in how to respond to the employers, and companies in how to deal with their customers. In part 4, we will apply what we call the "ETHICS Compass" to these work relationships.

The Old Testament book of Proverbs also offers much guidance on leadership, authority, partnerships, decision making, business and work ethics, goals, greed, integrity, money, peer pressure, profit, planning, scams, success, honesty, generosity, credit, client relations, and even marketing.

Conclusion

How did we lose our ethical way? We decided to do what is most convenient, what seems to further our careers, or what promises more things. And, after all, everyone else is taking the same ethical shortcuts. The reason we lost our ethical way is that we don't know how to choose the right thing to do. This has left us lost in the ethical wilderness at work.

We need to develop an ethical compass to guide us through the maze of work, to show God's standards as we deal with customers, co-workers, and company. Remember that a compass has fixed points: "north" is always north, and "south" is always south. Any ethical compass has fixed points—but we need to determine whose absolutes determine the directions. Where do these absolutes come from? You may even wonder whether there *are* moral absolutes.

To understand these questions, we must understand our moral foundation. That is the subject of the next chapter.

Developing an Ethics Compass

3

What Is Our Moral Foundation?

Shaky Pathway

On May 16, 2003, NBC's *Dateline* reported a story on bridge safety in the United States. Reporter Hoda Kotb and producer Andy Lehren found that, on average, "a barge or boat bangs into one of the nation's bridges every other day. Coast Guard records reveal that there have been more than 2,700 reports of vessels hitting bridges in 34 states in a recent 10-year period."[1]

One of the worst bridge disasters occurred on May 9, 1980, when the freighter *Summit Venture* hit the Sunshine Skyline bridge and knocked out a twelve-hundred-foot section of the bridge across the mouth of Tampa Bay. Thirty-five people—most of them passengers in a Greyhound bus—plunged 150 feet to their deaths.

Most of us probably do not want to consider the fact that the bridge over which we must pass could fail while we are on it. Not only are bridges subject to collapse because of neglected repairs, violent weather, and age, but they are also vulnerable to boat piloting errors. Many bridges we drive over have a shaky foundation.

That many people also have a shaky moral foundation can be seen in their decisions, priorities, and responses to circumstances. Watch them long enough and eventually their lives will come crashing down, like a bridge hit one too many times by a barge. To determine the proper ethical response at work, we must see what makes up our moral foundation. Where do values come from? Is there such a thing as a "moral law"? Are morals absolute and unchanging, or are they relative to the situation?

Answering these questions will give us the moral foundation needed, from which we can build a proper ethical response.

31

Where Do Values Originate?

In our book *Bringing Your Faith to Work* we discuss how our values are derived from the moral law.[2] The moral law deals with what is good versus what is evil. But every law that says we should do good and not do evil must have behind it a moral lawgiver. The evidence for a moral law is as follows:

1. *Every law has a lawgiver.* A moral law is a prescription—something we ought to do. But there is no prescription without a prescriber, no legislation without a legislator.
2. *There is a moral law.* Within the heart of every man, woman, and child, a law has been inscribed that drives our thoughts, reactions, and decisions. The moral law relates to a sense of morality that we are born with and to which we hold others accountable. Consider the following concepts.

The Concept of Fairness

Fairness is an internal awareness of how things should be, whether regarding children who have to do chores or people who feel a responsibility to protect the environment. Why should we do our part to save the environment? Why should we fight prejudice or feed the starving? Because we "ought" to, that's why. It's the "right thing to do." This sense of "ought" or fairness comes from a moral law written in our hearts. Moral laws don't *describe* what is; they *prescribe* what ought to be. They tell us what we ought to be doing, whether we are doing it or not.[3]

The Concept of Values

Consider the fact that certain values are found in virtually all human cultures.[4] Specific forms of killing are considered wrong in every culture. Lying and cheating and stealing are wrong. Where did this sense of moral right and wrong (law) come from?

The Concept of Accountability

Only people, not nature or animals, are judged as right and wrong. When a hurricane causes death and destruction, we don't describe it as "morally wrong." Laws governing natural forces as such do not morally discriminate. Gravity will kill anyone who jumps off of a high building. Animals are not judged wrong when they kill for food. Even when animals such as lions fight to establish social dominance, we don't say that is a wrong thing.

We hold people *accountable* for their actions because only people have the ability to make decisions based on what is right and wrong, and only they can understand the consequences of their actions.

The Concept of Guilt

Guilt is another indicator of ultimate right and wrong. We feel guilty when we violate a moral rule. One person called guilt "ethical pain."[5] Fairness, values, accountability, and guilt are all evidences of the moral law that is written on the heart of every person.

We have seen that every law has a lawgiver and that there is a moral law. That leads to our third point.

3. *Therefore, there is a moral lawgiver.* Where does fairness, that nagging sense of "ought," come from? The reason all human beings start out with an awareness of right and wrong and the reason we all yearn for justice and fairness is that we are made in the image of God, who is just and right. Romans 2:14–15 says that God has written this moral law in our hearts, as our conscience bears witness when we violate it. The reason we feel violated when someone "does us wrong" is that a moral law has been broken—and you can't have a moral law without a moral lawgiver. Every time you say or feel, "That's not fair!" you are testifying that there is a moral lawgiver.

Where do these values originate? The United States was founded on the concept that the moral law and values given by God are for every person. In the Declaration of Independence, by which colonial America declared itself free of English rule, Thomas Jefferson wrote that all men "are endowed by their Creator with certain unalienable rights." Jefferson believed that there is a moral law, which he called "nature's law that comes from 'Nature's God.'"

This is the basis of God-given human rights that are applicable to all people everywhere. Jefferson and the founding fathers understood that this moral law came from *the* moral Lawgiver—the "Creator." They believed that his moral law was the ultimate standard of right and wrong.[6]

How Do We Know the Moral Law Exists?

There are many ways we can know that the moral law exists.[7]

1. *The moral law is undeniable.* Relativists usually have two major positions: (1) either there is no absolute truth, or (2) there are no absolute values. A great tool for answering these objections is the "Road Runner" analogy, which applies each claim to itself. Most American adults remember the cartoon characters Road Runner and Wile E. Coyote. Coyote's only goal in life was to catch the Road Runner, who was too fast and too smart for him. Frequently the Coyote would miss Road Runner and find himself suspended in midair, supported by nothing. Soon he would go crashing down to the valley floor. That is what the

Road Runner tactic does to the relativists of our day: it helps them realize that their arguments have no support and fall to the ground.[8]

The Road Runner approach helps us to see that a self-defeating statement is one that fails to meet its own standard. Examples:

- "I can't speak a word in English." Didn't he say *that* in English?
- "Truth is not telling it like it is." Isn't *that* purporting to tell it like it is?
- "Opposites can both be true." Doesn't that mean that the opposite of *that* statement is true?
- "There is no truth." Then how is *that* true?
- "You can't know truth." So how do you know *that* is true? This is a self-defeating statement because it itself claims to be a known, absolute truth.
- "There is no absolute truth." Then is *that* absolutely true?
- "It's true for you but not for me." Is *that* just true for you but not for me? Try that one on your bank teller, the police, or the Internal Revenue Service when they collect taxes and see how far you get.

By turning a self-defeating statement on itself, you can expose it for the nonsense it is. It shows people that their arguments cannot sustain their own weight and plummet to the valley floor, just as Coyote did.

Like absolute truth, absolute values are undeniable. Even people who deny all values value their right to deny them. Not only that, but they want everyone else to value them as persons, even when they deny that people have value.

2. Our reactions reveal the moral law (right from wrong). If you want people to admit that a moral law exists, all you need to do is treat them unfairly. Their reactions will reveal the moral law that is written on their hearts and minds. The moral law is not always apparent from *actions*, as evidenced by the terrible things people do to each other. But it is clearly revealed in our *reactions*—what we do when we are treated unfairly. The moral law may not be the standard by which we treat others, but it is the standard by which we expect others to treat us. It does not describe how we behave, but it reveals how we *ought* to behave.

3. Without the moral law, we could not know justice or injustice. C. S. Lewis was once an atheist because he thought that if there was a good and loving God, then there would be no evil or injustice in the world. Then one day he thought about how he knew that the world was unjust. He wrote, "[As an atheist] my argument against God was that the universe seemed so cruel and unjust. But how had I got this idea of just and unjust? A man does not call a line crooked unless he has some idea of a straight line. What was I comparing this universe with when I called it unjust?"[9] This realization of a standard of morality led Lewis out of atheism and ultimately to Christianity.

In sum, we can't say something is unjust unless we know what is just. If there is anything that is absolutely unjust anywhere, then there must be an absolute moral lawgiver.

4. *Without the moral law, there would be no way to measure moral differences.* Who was a better person as measured by just treatment of others: Adolf Hitler or Mother Teresa?

Obviously, Mother Teresa was a much better person when it came to living justly than was Hitler. But how can you make that evaluation without basing it on objective, unchanging standards of morality and right and wrong to which both were subject? If the moral law does not exist, then there was no moral difference between Mother Teresa and Hitler.

Or answer the following questions: Is murder wrong? Is racism wrong? Is slavery wrong? Is abusing children wrong? If you answered "Yes," then on what basis did you come up with those answers? The logical end of moral relativism is that there are no differences between Mother Teresa and Hitler, freedom and slavery, abuse and care, or life and murder. Such conclusions are absurd, so moral relativism must be false. It is false because an objective moral law exists.

5. *Without the moral law, we would not make excuses for violating it.* Isn't it interesting that people make excuses for their immoral behavior? Nearly every person arrested seems to have an excuse for their criminal behavior. Making excuses, whether from adults or children, is clear evidence that the moral law exists. Why make excuses if no behavior is immoral? We only make excuses when we act against the moral law. We would not do so if it did not exist.

6. *Without the moral law, we could not measure moral progress.* We make statements such as, "The world is getting better." But we can't know *better* unless we know what is *best*. We can't measure moral progress or regress without an absolute standard beyond society by which we measure it.

Absolute vs. Relative: Why the Confusion?

If there is a moral law, then why do so many believe that morality is relative? Why do people appear to have such different values? Is it because of culture, conditioning, or something else? People today are confused about whether morals are absolute or relative.[10]

Confusion 1: Absolute Morals vs. Changing Behavior

Relativists commonly mistake behavior with values. They confuse what *is* with what *ought* to be. What people *do* is subject to change, but what they *ought* to do is not. Relativists, then, often confuse the changing behavioral situation with the unchanging moral duty.

For example, the attitude toward sexual immorality has changed drastically in the past forty years. Beginning in the late 1960s, the concept of "free love" began to reign on college campuses, on the radio, and in young people's behavior. The teachings of the free love movement became "Make love, not war" and "If it feels good, do it." Those advocating a similar philosophy now use the reasoning, "This is the twenty-first century, not the Victorian century." This movement once was called the "sexual revolution," a revolution against the moral law of not engaging in sex until marriage and remaining married to one person for life.

Since this revolution took hold, we have seen the increase of sexually transmitted diseases, including the arrival of HIV/AIDS, plus unwanted pregnancies resulting in abortions by the millions. Now, desperate public school systems are looking for ways to get across the message of abstinence, having one partner, and waiting until marriage to have sex. Among the seven in ten public school districts that have a districtwide policy to teach sexuality education, the majority (86 percent) require that abstinence be promoted as the *preferred* option for teenagers (51 percent teach "abstinence plus") or as the *only* option outside of marriage (35 percent teach "abstinence-only"), according to a study by the Alan Guttmacher Institute.[11]

Western society is finally beginning to admit that sexual immorality is not right, while the absolute of sexual fidelity, which is written in our hearts, is the only way to protect ourselves physically, emotionally, and spiritually.

Confusion 2: Absolute Morals vs. Changing Perceptions of the Facts

Some people confuse the absolute moral value itself with the understanding of the facts used in applying that value. C. S. Lewis pointed out that in the late 1700s witches were treated as murderers, but now they are not.[12] A relativist would point out that since we no longer seek to kill witches, our moral values have changed; thus morality is relative to time and culture.

But look more carefully. What has changed is not the moral *principle* that murder is wrong. What changed was the *perception* that witches can murder people by their curses. The perception of a moral situation is relative (whether witches are really murderers), but the moral values involved in the situation are not (murder has always been and always will be wrong).

Confusion 3: Absolute Morals vs. Application to Particular Situations

What happens when people view the same situation but disagree over the morality of a decision regarding it, such as whether a convicted criminal should receive a death sentence or life in prison? Does disagreement mean that morality is relative to different people or situations?

An absolute moral law can exist even if people fail to know the right thing to do in a particular situation. While people may get confused over morality in complicated issues, such as the death penalty, they get it right with the basics. Even Hitler knew murder was wrong. That's why he had to dehumanize the Jews in order to get support for their extermination. Cannibals appear to know that it is wrong to kill innocent human beings, which is why they perform elaborate ceremonies to dehumanize their victims.[13] Truthfully answering the simple moral question, "Is murder justified?" proves that at least *one* moral law exists. If just one moral law exists (such as "Don't murder," "Don't rape," or "Don't torture babies"), then the moral law exists. If the moral law exists, then the moral Lawgiver exists as well.

Confusion 4: Absolute Morals vs. Moral Disagreements

The hot topic of abortion seems to prove to relativists that morality is relative. Some think abortion is acceptable while others see it as murder. Yet the basis of the abortion controversy exists because each side is fighting over an absolute moral value—protecting life versus protecting liberty (a woman being in control of her own body). The controversy is over which absolute value takes priority in the issue of abortion.[14] If the unborn are not human beings, then a woman's choice should take precedence. But if the unborn are human beings, then one person's liberty is not more important than another's life. The baby is not just part of a woman's body; the baby has his or her own body with a unique genetic code, blood type, and gender. Even if we doubt when life begins, the benefit should be given to protecting life. Police officers are trained not to shoot their weapons if they might accidentally injure or kill an innocent bystander. The moral disagreement over the topic of abortion exists because some people suppress the moral law to justify what they want to do.

Confusion 5: Absolute Ends (Values) vs. Relative Means

Many times relativists confuse the end (the value itself) with the means to attaining that end. Both sides on political disagreements can desire the same things, the same *ends*; they just disagree on the best means to attain them. For example, everyone wants to help alleviate poverty. The debate is about what is the best means to accomplish this.

Conclusion

We have become lost in the ethical wilderness at work because we don't know what makes up our moral foundation. We have learned that our moral foundation, our values, come from the moral law that is given to all by the moral Lawgiver. We have also seen that morality is not relative to the situation but rather is absolute—for all people of all times in all places. Knowing this gives us the moral foundation from which we can build a proper ethical response.

From this moral foundation comes our ethics, the decisions that we make in difficult situations. This leads to very important questions: What is ethics? What is a Christian view of ethics? What are the various views on ethical dilemmas? And what is the best procedure for deciding between right and wrong?

To understand the answers to these questions, we must examine the concept of ethics carefully. That is the subject of the next chapter.

4

What Is Ethics?

Résumé Padding

Both of us authors have conducted a lot of interviews and hired many applicants. As one evaluates a candidate's résumé, questions begin to arise: "Does the candidate have a criminal background? Does he or she have a hidden drug problem? Has this person lied about credentials?"

There is a good reason for suspicion. In 2002, *HR* magazine reported that 10 to 20 percent of applicants blatantly lie to prospective employers, 12.6 percent do not disclose a criminal conviction, and 23 to 30 percent lie about their employment history or education credentials.[1] In another survey by the *New York Times* Job Market, a research team found that 89 percent of job seekers and 49 percent of hiring managers in the New York metropolitan area believe that "most people" pad their résumés.[2]

Think these statistics are too high to be accurate? Consider some notable examples:

- *I can see clearly now.* For ten years, Bausch & Lomb CEO Ronald Zarella lied about having an MBA. When the lie was revealed in 2002, Zarella lied again, but the company kept him on. Zarella had not completed his degree requirements at New York University.[3]
- *What is truth?* Kenneth Lonchar was CFO of Veritas Software, a successful Silicon Valley firm. It was discovered in 2002 that he had lied about

39

his Stanford University MBA and his undergraduate education.[4] *Veritas*, interestingly enough, means "truth" in Latin.

- *The Big Blue is blue.* Jeffrey Papows, chairman of Lotus, a $1.4 billion subsidiary of IBM, made up several facts about his life, including a PhD degree and a martial arts black belt. Although Papows allegedly told business associates that he was an orphan, his parents live in Massachusetts.[5]
- *Go for the gold.* Sandra Baldwin, the first woman president of the United States Olympic Committee, resigned in 2002 after it was revealed that she had lied about having a PhD in English from Arizona State University.[6]
- *Fighting Irish?* In 2001, George O'Leary shocked the collegiate football world when he was forced to resign five days after being hired as head coach of Notre Dame University's football team. He admitted that he had falsely claimed to have a master's degree from New York University. He also claimed to have lettered in football for three years when in fact he had not played in a single game.[7]
- *Radio Shack's shock.* In February 2006, Radio Shack's president and CEO, David Edmonson, resigned after admitting that he had lied when he claimed that he earned two college degrees in theology and psychology from a school that he attended for only two semesters. The school has never offered a degree in psychology.[8]

Why would people make false claims when one phone call to an educational institution will uncover their deception? Let's consider again the reasons for unethical decisions listed in chapter 2:

Relinquishing occurs when we say, for example, that we graduated from a more prestigious institution or earned a more valued degree than is the case. Positioning, which is common in the workplace, is when we try to position ourselves ahead of the competition by telling from what school we graduated, what degrees we have, how big our business is, and how important our role is. Sometimes we are tempted to stretch the truth to sound more impressive. Before we know it, the lie has grown so big that we fear we cannot go back and tell the truth. So we do what is most convenient—nothing.

Résumé thinking tells us that we need to do whatever it takes to get ahead professionally. Deception may work, but only for a time. The old saying, "Pay me now or pay me later" certainly applies here. Lying can lead to *rewards* in prestigious positions, phenomenal salaries, all the toys money can buy, and the accolades of men. For a time the people who practice such deception may think they are getting away with it and that their deception is worth it. They may rationalize by lying to themselves, "Everyone else does it, so why not?"

But this is not an excuse, and it is not true. Most people actually go to school and earn their degrees. *Rationalizing* is what people do in the quiet hours of the night when the gremlins of guilt and fear gnaw at their souls.

How do people who have told lies to get ahead fight the midnight gremlins of conscience and fear of discovery? Do they sleep? One night in the spring of 2002, Quincy Troupe, a prolific poet and professor at the University of California in San Diego, received news that should have meant the crowning achievement of his career. A phone call informed him that he was one of three finalists for the honor of becoming the first poet laureate recognized by the state of California.

But Troupe was not excited about the honor. "At that moment, when I hung the phone up, I thought . . . 'Oh, man. This is not cool.'"

Despite all his achievements, Troupe lacked a college diploma. That would not have been a problem, except that for twenty-six years Troupe had listed a bachelor's degree from Grambling College (now Grambling State University) on his curriculum vitae. He claimed to have graduated in 1963, but he had not finished a single semester.

Troupe was chosen to be the first poet laureate for California. His worst fears were realized four months later when a routine background check turned up the lie. Confronted with the facts, Troupe immediately resigned as poet laureate. When informed that the university might suspend him for up to a year without pay, he retired.

He said he had thought about removing the false degree from the record, but "it's a Gordian knot. How do you undo it?"[9] William Shakespeare said, "Suspicion always haunts the guilty mind; the thief doth fear each bush an officer."[10]

How can we live in such a way that we don't fear being found out? How can we have what the Bible calls a "clear conscience" (Acts 24:16) and avoid making an unethical decision? The answer is that we must make our choices based on an ethical lifestyle.

Ethics Defined

Ethics can be defined as "what is morally right and wrong. *Christian ethics* deals with what is morally right and wrong for a Christian."[11] Living ethically as a Christian means being the "salt of the earth" (Matt. 5:13) where the Lord has placed us. "Preservation of meat and fish was one of the most extensive uses of salt in [Jesus's] day."[12] Jesus was salt to the moral decay of his world, and he expects his church to be as well.

As salt, Christians slow the world's decay and moral corruption by demonstrating a life of integrity before unbelievers. In the workplace, that means we must shake Christ's salt on the moral wounds that we encounter. We must refuse to go along with those who want to lie, cheat, or steal. And we may have to stand up and confront those who are leading others astray. Moreover, we will have to resolve ethical dilemmas and difficulties in a biblical manner.

Yes, the Bible does give us guidance for making ethical decisions, especially in the workplace! The bottom line is that *salt is integrity—doing the right thing at all times no matter what*. Making the right choices no matter who comes with us. Taking a stand against evil even if we must do so alone and suffer the consequences. If our saltiness remains unpoured or is washed away by a lack of integrity or poor work effort, we have become useless.[13]

A Christian View of Ethics

How can we be the salt of the earth, living ethically at work? Five characteristics distinguish Christian ethics.[14]

1. Christian Ethics Is Based on God's Will.

As we saw in chapter 2, whatever action God specifies as good is good and whatever action God specifies as evil is evil. This forms the basis for a Christian ethic. Christian ethics is a form of the divine-command position. This means that we ought to fulfill an ethical duty because God, the source of all good, commands us to do so.

2. Christian Ethics Is Absolute.

Since God's moral character does not change (2 Tim. 2:13; Heb. 6:18), moral obligations flowing from his nature are *absolute*: they are always binding everywhere on everyone. Take, for example, God's command not to murder. It was applied before the Law was given to Moses (Gen. 9:6), under the law of Moses (Exod. 20:13), and since the time of Moses (Rom. 13:9). Murder is wrong at all times in all places and for all people. Humans are created in the "image and likeness of God" (Gen. 1:27; 9:6), which includes a moral likeness to God (Col. 3:10; James 3:9). Therefore, whatever is traceable to God's unchanging moral character is a moral absolute. This includes moral obligations such as holiness, justice, love, truthfulness, and mercy. Absolute moral duties are binding on all people at all times and in all places.

3. Christian Ethics Is Based on God's Revelation.

Christian ethics is based on God's revealed commands. Part of this revelation is *general* in that God has revealed himself to us through nature (Ps. 19:1–6; Rom. 1:19–20; 2:12–15). Part of this revelation is also *special* in that God has revealed himself in Scripture (Ps. 19:7–14; Rom. 2:18; 3:2).

General revelation unveils God's commands for all people, as found in the moral law (Rom. 2:14–15). Special revelation declares his will for believers, revealed to us through the inspired writers of Scripture. In both cases, the basis of human ethical responsibility is divine revelation.

Failure to recognize God as the source of moral duty does not exonerate people from their moral duty, not even atheists. Regardless of whether people believe in God, lying, cheating, stealing, and murder are still wrong. For "when Gentiles, who do not have the law [of Moses], do by nature things required by the law, they are a law for themselves, even though they do not have the law, since they show the requirements of the law written in their hearts" (Rom. 2:14–15). If unbelievers do not have the moral law on their minds, they still have it written on their hearts. Even if they do not know it by way of cognition, they show it by way of inclination. Thus they are without excuse.

4. Christian Ethics Is Prescriptive.

Since moral rightness is prescribed by a moral God, it is binding. For there is no moral law without a moral lawgiver, no moral legislation without a moral legislator. So Christian ethics is, by its very nature, prescriptive rather than descriptive. That is, ethics deals with what ought to be, not with what is. Christians do not find their ethical duties in the standard *of* Christians but in the standard *for* Christians—the Bible.

5. Christian Ethics Is Duty-Centered.

There are basically two major categories of ethical systems—duty-centered (deontological) and end-centered (teleological). Christian ethics is duty-centered in that ethical duty to God underlies decisions or rules for living. This word comes from the Greek word *deon*, which means "binding duty."[15] The teleological approach is utilitarian and believes that the results of life determine the rules for life.

The following chart summarizes the differences between these two approaches.

Duty-centered (Deontological) Ethics	End-centered (Teleological) Ethics
Rule determines the result.	Result determines the rule.
Rule is the basis of the act.	Result is the basis for the act.
Rule is good regardless of result.	Rule is good because of result.
Result must be measured within the rules.	Results sometimes justify breaking the rules.

When Randy's wife, Kris, a registered nurse, was studying to take her critical care nursing certification exam, it was interesting to note that her 2000 edition critical care nursing textbook had a chapter on ethical practice. This chapter discussed various approaches to making ethical decisions, such as deontology, teleology, utilitarianism, egoism, paternalism, obligationism, social contract theory, and natural law.

The book defined *deontology* as an approach that considers actions as right or wrong based on a set of morals or rules. This approach, emphasizing duty or obligation, was regarded by the textbook's authors as the "only acceptable ethical theory for decision making in health care."[16] Since they deal with life-and-death dilemmas every day, most people in the health care industry recognize the value of duty-centered ethics.

Various Views of Ethical Conflicts

Realistically, maintaining moral absolutes involves problems. What do you do when two or more moral principles come into conflict? There are six major ethical systems, each identified by its answer to the question, "Are there any absolute moral laws that are binding on all humans at all times?"[17]

1. *Antinomianism* says there are no moral laws, absolute or relative.
2. *Situationism* affirms there is one absolute law (love).
3. *Generalism* claims there are some general laws but no absolute ones.
4. *Unqualified absolutism* assumes there are many absolute laws that never conflict.
5. *Conflicting absolutism* contends there are many absolute norms that sometimes conflict, and we are obligated to do the lesser evil.
6. *Greater good*, or *graded*, *absolutism*, holds to many absolute laws that sometimes conflict, and we are responsible for obeying the higher law.

Of the six basic ethical views, two deny all objective absolute moral laws. Antinomianism denies all universal and general moral laws. Generalism, on the other hand, denies only universal moral laws but holds to general ones. In other words, there are some objective moral laws that are binding most of the time but not necessarily all of the time.

Joseph Fletcher's situationism accepts only one absolute—love—which cannot be defined in advance of the situation. "Since Christian ethics is firmly rooted in the unchanging moral character of God (Lev. 11:45; Mal. 3:6), the first three options are not for the Christian."[18] The Christian must decide from the remaining three options that hold to the existence of absolute moral laws.

- *Ostrich approach*. Unqualified absolutism, or the "ostrich" approach, contends that absolute moral principles never conflict. Persons who believe that moral conflicts are only apparent are like the proverbial ostrich that sticks its head in the sand. They contend that since most moral actions are right or wrong and because sin is always avoidable, there can be no moral conflict. They believe that God will always provide an alternative to sinful actions.

- *Lesser of Two Evils approach.* Conflicting absolutism, or the "Lesser of Two Evils" approach believes that moral principles do sometimes conflict. This viewpoint contends that we are responsible to do the lesser evil but are guilty of whichever commandment we break.
- *Greater Good approach.* Graded absolutism holds that our responsibility is to obey the greater commandment, and we are not guilty for not following the lesser conflicting commandment. Many Christians agree there is a basic gradation or hierarchy of values that places God over people and people over things. When there is a conflict between two levels in the hierarchy, the higher takes precedence. So, we should love God more than people, and we should love people over things.[19]

The Greater Good Approach

Understanding the Greater Good approach is essential to making ethical decisions, as the rest of this book will show. We start with its three essential premises.[20]

There Are Higher and Lower Moral Laws

Not all moral laws are of equal weight (Matt. 5:19; 23:23; John 15:13; 19:11). The other two Christian positions admit this but do not have a justification for such a belief. Examples of these higher and lower laws:

- *Love God more than people.* Loving God is the greatest and highest commandment (Matt. 22:36–38). In fact, Jesus said that our love for God should be so strong that our love for parents would look like hate by contrast (Luke 14:26).
- *Love people more than things.* We should never view the things of this world as treasures and treat people as toys (Matt. 22:39; 1 Tim. 6:17–19). Lying to gain things in business is wrong.
- *Love others more than self.* Matthew 7:12, sometimes called the Golden Rule, sets a strong pattern for business decisions. Asking, "How would I feel if I were in their shoes?" reveals the loving and ethical thing to do in most situations.
- *Obey God over government.* Generally we are to submit to and obey the government (Rom. 13:1–2; Titus 3:1). There are times, however, when disobedience to government is the higher moral law and is approved by God (Daniel 6; Acts 5:29). For example, we must disobey if a government

tries to force us into false worship (Daniel 3), commands us not to worship (Daniel 6), or tells us we cannot preach the gospel (Acts 4–5). And we must not obey a government's commands to murder the innocent (Exodus 1).

There Are Unavoidable Moral Conflicts

Unavoidable moral conflicts occur when an individual faces two commands and cannot obey both. This is when the hierarchy helps, and the higher takes precedence over the lower. Several examples might be cited from the Bible, but one will suffice. Abraham knew God's command not to murder. Then he was commanded by God to kill his only son (Gen. 22:1–2). Abraham chose to kill his son (Heb. 11:17, 19), yet he chose without sin (James 2:21). He was a godly man in a dilemma: he had to choose between two unavoidable, absolute commandments. He followed the higher law.

No Guilt Is Imputed for the Unavoidable

Abraham was not held guilty for his decision but instead was commended for it (Heb. 11:17–19). God does not hold individuals responsible for the personally unavoidable moral conflicts they face, as long as they keep the higher law. Logically, a just God will not hold a person responsible for doing what is actually impossible, such as avoiding the unavoidable! Therefore, a person is not morally responsible; instead, God grants an exemption to the lower in view of our duty to obey the higher.

Is Greater Good (Graded Absolutism) Really Absolute?

If obedience to lower commands is sometimes unnecessary, then how can we call this ethical system an absolutism? First, the moral laws are absolute as to their *source* (God). Second, each moral law is absolute in its *sphere*. For example, lying is always wrong except when it conflicts with saving a life. Third, each moral law is absolute in its *priority*. That is, the hierarchy of values is set up by God in accordance with his nature and is therefore absolute. God has established that he is first, persons are next, and things are last.

Conclusion

We began by looking at successful people who padded their résumés for personal gain, such as to advance in their careers. They managed to justify their own lies because they did not have an ethical lifestyle. The Christian develops an ethical lifestyle by practicing what is morally right in terms of what God wills. What God wills is based on his moral nature. Since his moral nature does not change, the moral obligations flowing from his nature are absolute and are binding on all people everywhere.

Christian ethics then is based on God's absolutes, which demand our duty-centered obedience. When the various views of ethical absolutes are evaluated, the Greater Good system is the most logical and biblical approach. The Greater Good approach will be seen to be a key element in developing an ethical lifestyle.

How can we make all of this theoretical information practical for the workplace? This book is not a textbook to stimulate hypothetical discussions in a classroom. It is a field manual for those on the front lines of the battlefield—the workplace. Our intention is to develop an approach to an ethical lifestyle that actually guides us in making the right decisions. In the next chapter we reveal a tool to point us in the right direction: the ETHICS compass.

5

The ETHICS Compass

The Loneliness of Integrity

When President Abraham Lincoln was assassinated on April 14, 1865, he was carrying several items in his pockets. The Library of Congress first displayed those items in 1976: a handkerchief embroidered with "A. Lincoln," a country boy's penknife, spectacles with a lens polisher, a pocket watch, a brown wallet containing a five-dollar bill in Confederate currency, and some worn newspaper clippings.[1]

Most interesting are the newspaper clippings that Lincoln kept so close. Each is an article that describes his accomplishments and personal attributes. One has the text of a speech by John Bright, a British statesman. Bright praised Lincoln as a man of focused purpose, unfaltering patriotism, and a "brightness of personal honor" in his execution of presidential duties. He was a man that no adversary has been able to stain, and whose reelection was crucial to the future of the United States.

Bright's assessment is commonly shared today, but in 1865 the critics of the president were fierce and many. His decisions, it was charged, had led the country into war and kept the country at war. This cruel and costly war ripped the country apart as brother fought against brother. As the war dragged on, many in the North began to wonder if the cost of providing freedom to slaves was worth it and whether the president really knew what he was doing. During the 1864 presidential election campaign, public opinion had so turned against Lincoln that he seriously doubted that he would be reelected. Thus he drafted a contingency plan for the transfer of power of the presidency.[2]

48

Those newspaper clippings found on the body of Lincoln speak volumes of his lonely agony and internal struggle with the decisions he faced. One can almost see this great leader seeking peace and surety from these few newspaper stories as he reads them again and again under the flickering flame of an oil lamp, all alone in his office.

Lincoln's unswerving stand against slavery had divided a nation and turned his own party, even some of his own cabinet, against him. Yet he would not back down and compromise over the subject of slavery, even though this was deemed the "politically correct" thing to do and something the 1864 Democratic Party nominee, George McClellan, swore he would do. Many, such as Henry Raymond, editor and owner of the *New York Times*, a pro-Lincoln paper, strongly pressured Lincoln to negotiate peace with Jefferson Davis, president of the Southern Confederacy, over the slavery issue in order to get reelected.[3]

How did Lincoln come to make a decision in opposing slavery that seemed wrong at the time but right for the ages? How was he so sure that this decision was right that he was willing to lose an election rather than compromise his stand? A moral compass guided Lincoln to make the most difficult decision of his career.

Harper's Weekly saw Abraham Lincoln as a man with such a steady moral compass that he would not give in to extremists on either side. An editorial in May 1862 said, "In the President of the United States Providence has vouch-safed a leader whose moral perceptions are blinded neither by sophistry nor enthusiasm—who knows that permanent results must grow, and can not be prematurely seized."[4]

How can we have a moral standard that is not influenced by outside forces?

In chapter 1 we pointed out the necessity of having a moral compass to guide us through the ethical wilderness of work. First, without a compass we are lost, for we have strayed from the right path of morality. Second, a compass has fixed points—north is always north and south is always south. Only by following these fixed points will we find our way. We learned in chapters 3 and 4 that God, through his Word, gives us absolutes, or fixed points. They are as fixed as north being north and south being south. Third, a compass is a directional tool to show us the right way. The important thing is to find these fixed points, or absolutes, to keep us going the right way.

It used to be that people were raised with values that helped set the compass. For honest businesspeople, your word was your bond; a handshake was enough to seal a deal. Throughout society, children were taught to be polite and respectful. Men tipped their hats to women, opened doors for them, and took their hats off for the national anthem. Women knew the code of conduct required to be a "lady." To the generation now in the workplace, those social mores seem as archaic as the medical practices of the 1700s.

Before a house can be built, one must first build the foundation. Before a foundation can be built, the ground must be cleared. But the workplace today is filled with people, including many who identify themselves as Christians, who are relativistic in all areas of life. There are Christians in the workplace who live out a dichotomy separating Sunday from Monday through Friday. On Sunday they are Christians, living by absolutes of God. But when the work week starts, they "go with the flow."

To build a foundation, we must go back and teach why absolutism is the only correct approach. First, we must clear the land, as we did in chapter 1. The foundation for ethics was poured in chapters 2 through 4. In this chapter, we will build the framework of the house, using the ETHICS Compass. Then in chapters 6 through 8, we will finish construction by showing how the ETHICS Compass worked in the book of Daniel. In chapters 9 through 13, we will show how to live in the house by applying the ETHICS Compass to practical areas of the workplace in which people have asked for help (as in the survey in chapter 1). We will cover sexual ethics, issues applicable to employers, issues applicable to employees, and issues applicable to customers.

A compass is needed to guide people in making ethical decisions in the marketplace. The compass must be easy to understand and follow. Finding such an existing guide for making decisions is nearly impossible. So we have summarized teachings of the Bible in a guide called the ETHICS Compass. Here is why we commend it as a tool:

- The ETHICS Compass is a step-by-step guide to making ethical decisions. Ethical decisions have short-term, long-term, and eternal consequences, so we had better get them right. The steps to making proper decisions must be followed sequentially. The ETHICS Compass is a practical resource that guides you through the successive steps.
- The ETHICS Compass is an acrostic, so it is more easily understood and memorable. Sometimes you have days, even weeks, to make a difficult decision. At other times, you have one hour. As you sit in your office staring at the wall, you can remember the steps of the ETHICS Compass.
- The ETHICS Compass takes into account ethical concepts that are necessary to consider when making a decision. This compass guides you to ethical wisdom found in Scripture to enable you to consider consequences, explore alternatives, understand the greater good, and receive wisdom as given by the Holy Spirit.

A summary of the ETHICS compass is as follows:

E—Examine the Facts. Before you make a decision, make sure you have all of the facts in front of you.

T—(Seek the) Truth. Seek wisdom from God through prayer and the Bible.

H—Hesitate. Determine if there is anything about your decision that makes you hesitate before proceeding.

I—Identify the Greater Good. There is a hierarchy of values that places God over people and people over things. Whenever there is an unavoidable conflict, the higher takes precedence over the lower.

C—Consider Consequences and Creative Alternatives. Think through the consequences of your decision and any creative alternatives you can develop to wrong directives.

S—Stand for God. Knowing that suffering for God leads to glory, purpose to stand for God no matter what.

Let's see how the ETHICS Compass works.

E—Examine the Facts

When making a proper ethical decision, make sure you have all of the facts, then examine them carefully.

"Well, of course you need to first examine the facts," someone might say with a sarcastic laugh. "That's so obvious. Everyone knows that."

In our many years of counseling experience, we have found that people very often make important decisions without considering *all* of the facts. Even for such issues as marital difficulties, spiritual wisdom, workplace decisions, and career guidance, individuals come to us with their minds made up, simply wanting us to rubber-stamp their decision. As we explore the rationale for their decision, we find that they have not considered all of the facts. Other times, people are lost and don't know what to do because they have made unwarranted assumptions or are acting on false information.

When we make decisions without knowing all of the facts, we do so at our peril. The Bible gives us the following wisdom:

- *Understanding the facts will win praise from others.* "Good understanding wins favor, but the way of the unfaithful is hard" (Prov. 13:15).
- *Understanding brings blessing, but a lack of understanding only produces folly.* "Understanding is a fountain of life to those who have it, but folly brings punishment to fools" (Prov. 16:22).
- *Get all the facts before you respond.* "He who answers before listening—that is his folly and his shame" (Prov. 18:13).
- *Be diligent in developing your plans, and they will be profitable.* "The plans of the diligent lead to profit as surely as haste leads to poverty" (Prov. 21:5).

- *Count the cost before you do anything.* "Suppose one of you wants to build a tower. Will he not first sit down and estimate the cost to see if he has enough money to complete it?" (Luke 14:28).

The general implication of these texts is that you should not move forward until you know what is required of you and why. Be thorough in your fact-finding until you know all the relevant facts. If you are unsure of a decision, get counsel from knowledgeable friends. If you are being asked to do something questionable by a customer or your boss, ask all of the questions you can.

Lincoln made sure he knew the facts. "During his four years as president Abraham Lincoln spent most of his time among the troops," according to Donald Phillips in his study of Lincoln as leader.[5] To hear the latest information on the war effort, Lincoln walked from the White House to Secretary of War Edwin M. Stanton's office nearly every day. During critical battles Lincoln made the trip two or three times a day. He even spent one night on the sofa of the telegraph office waiting for news from the front. Phillips observes:

> Rather than haunting the War Department's Telegraph Office, Lincoln could have waited in the White House for a messenger to bring him word of progress in key battles. But he preferred to be right there, peering over the shoulder of the decoder and getting the information as fast as it came in. This put Lincoln in a position where he could make quick decisions with virtually no delay.[6]

One of the best ways to ask questions and make sure you have all of the necessary facts is to use the "rephrasing" technique. One of the authors teaches conflict resolution skills in a seminar titled "Office Zoo."[7] In this seminar, the different "animals" we face at work are identified and then the key "taming tools" are taught. These tools help to tame our animals when they are being difficult and then train them to keep them from attacking in the future. These concepts have been taught for years and have been effective in resolving conflict, whether in the secular workplace, a church, or a marriage.

One of these taming tools is the "rephrasing" technique. Rephrasing is a key taming tool that helps us really listen to another person. Listening to people is a difficult skill, especially when we are being told something that we do not want to hear. When involved in a disagreement, we respond to what we *thought* we heard the other person say. From that perceived meaning, we develop our own scenario of what the person wants from us, which may or may not be accurate.

Psychologist Gary Smalley calls this communication technique "drive-through talking."[8] In America, ordering food from one's car in the "drive-thru lane" at a fast-food restaurant is a common experience. You place your order by speaking into a two-way intercom. The clerk inside the restaurant listens to your order, writes it down, then repeats it for you to hear. If you agree, you say, "Yes," and then proceed. If the clerk missed a detail, you repeat the order until it is right.

Rephrasing aids communication with the same three steps used at the restaurant:

1. *Share.* Let the person share his or her point of view.
2. *Repeat.* Repeat in your own words what you think the other person means. "Let me make sure that I heard you correctly. Did you say that I should do . . . ?"
3. *Agree.* If the other person says, "No," continue to rephrase until there is agreement. Now you have listened, and the other person knows you have listened.

This is a major step to making sure that you have at your fingertips all of the correct facts from which to make a proper decision.

T—(Seek the) Truth

The second step in making a proper ethical decision is to listen to God: What does the Bible have to say about the issue? Is it "black and white," with the Bible clearly saying, "Thou shalt not"? Or is it more of a "gray" issue that the Bible doesn't specifically address? If the Bible seems to be unclear, there are steps to follow in seeking God's will in Scripture.

First, seek wisdom from the Bible. The Bible is the best business guidance book you can read. The book of Proverbs has so many things to say about business success that we have provided an appendix at the end of this book, listing them.

Lincoln got his guidance for leading our nation from the important truths of the Bible. A Bible in the Fisk University Library, Nashville, Tennessee, is inscribed: "To Abraham Lincoln, President of the United States, the Friend of Universal Freedom, from the Loyal Colored People of Baltimore, as a token of respect and Gratitude. Baltimore, 4th July 1864." Lincoln was actually presented the Bible in Washington on September 7, 1864, with the donors using a memorable phrase as they presented the handsome Bible: "Since our incorporation into the American family, we have been true and loyal."

Lincoln's response to this moving presentation clearly revealed his respect for the Holy Scriptures. "In regard to this Great book," he replied, "I have but to say, it is the best gift God has given to man. All the good Savior gave to the world was communicated through this book. But for it we could not know right from wrong. All things most desirable for man's welfare, here and hereafter, are to be found portrayed in it. To you I return my most sincere thanks for the elegant copy of the great Book of God which you present."[9]

It may seem that using Lincoln's relationship with God could be troublesome since it is a subject debated by historians today. Some say Lincoln was an unbeliever or skeptic—a deist at best. Others claim that he was deeply religious and daily sought God's guidance.

The primary reason for the debate is information in a biography of Lincoln written by William Herndon, Lincoln's young law partner in Springfield, Illinois. The biography, published in 1889, proclaimed Lincoln to be an "infidel." There is no doubt that the young lawyer Herndon had known went through a period of doubt about the truth of Christianity. But Herndon refused to acknowledge that his friend had become settled in his faith over the years.

It is true that Lincoln never joined a church, but only 23 percent of people in the United States were church members in 1860, compared to 60 percent in 1960.[10] Lincoln did attend church services regularly while president. The reason he gave for never joining a church was that he could never be satisfied with all the dogmas and creeds the denominational churches of his day required. Mrs. Lincoln said that after their son Willy died in early 1862, her husband drew much closer to God.

As early as 1846, Lincoln expressed at least a warm regard for Christianity:

> That I am not a member of any Christian church is true; but I have never denied the truth of the Scriptures; and I have never spoken with intentional disrespect of religion in general, or of any denomination of Christians in particular. I do not think I could myself be brought to support a man for office whom I knew to be an open enemy of, or scoffer at, religion.[11]

When one reads in Lincoln's presidential speeches his pleas to the American people to seek God and his guidance, and reads his descriptions of his own dependence on God and his Word, it is difficult to understand how any scholar could see Lincoln as anything but a man who sincerely depended on God.

The evidence is strong that Lincoln did look to the Bible for guidance in making leadership decisions. When facing decisions in the workplace, we, too, should seek wisdom from the Bible.

Second, pray for wisdom, and God will grant it. The apostle Paul writes, "For this reason, since the day we heard about you, we have not stopped praying for you and asking God to fill you with the knowledge of his will through all spiritual wisdom and understanding" (Col. 1:9). James advises, "If any of you lacks wisdom, he should ask God, who gives generously to all without finding fault, and it will be given to him" (James 1:5).

Lincoln prayed to God for wisdom in making difficult decisions. David Elton Trueblood writes: "The evidence of Abraham Lincoln's own practice of personal prayer is so abundant that no thoughtful person can deny it. He prayed alone, and he called the nation to prayer; he prayed for guidance, and he prayed in gratitude; he prayed in defeat, and he prayed in victory. Often noted was his reverence when others engaged in vocal prayer."[12]

Noah Brooks, personal friend and biographer of Lincoln, reported that the president, after entering the White House and in spite of the demands of a busy schedule, observed daily the practice of prayer. "Sometimes," said Brooks, "it was only ten words, but those ten words he had."[13]

If Lincoln recognized his need to pray for guidance, so should we. The Bible declares that as God's children we will be led by the Holy Spirit (Rom. 8:14; Gal. 5:18). The Holy Spirit delights to reveal his will to his seeking children. First Kings 19:12 says that God speaks to us in a "still small voice" (KJV), or a "gentle whisper" (NIV). When struggling with a decision, seek the Lord.

When our ethical dilemma has a black-and-white solution clearly spelled out by the Bible, what do we do next? And what about dilemmas that are gray areas? These questions lead to our next step.

H—Hesitate

A traffic light gives us guidance as we approach an intersection. The green light means it is okay to proceed through the intersection; the red light means we must stop because other lanes of traffic have the right of way. Some people think that the yellow light means to speed up to make it through the intersection before the light turns red. But that's not the case. The yellow light is the caution signal to slow down rather than speed up. The *hesitate* step is the yellow caution light we see at the intersection of a difficult ethical decision.

This third step in making a proper ethical decision asks whether there is anything about our decision that should be considered before proceeding. What do we do when we settle on a course of action but then sense a "red flag" or a "little voice" whispering to us to slow down or stop altogether? Is this just the fear of doing the right thing, or is our conscience trying to tell us something?

First, we should ask, "Why am I hesitating? Am I hesitating because I know what the Bible says to do but I don't know *how* to do it?" Uncertainty about the next step can paralyze us much like a deer caught in the headlights of an oncoming car. More frequently we know what the Bible says to do, but we are *afraid* of what will happen if we do it. Seeing the consequences of our proposed action, we can be paralyzed with fear. We can be afraid of our boss, the loss of a job, the loss of privilege, or even the loss of our house. When fear of consequences for doing what is right begins to immobilize us in the workplace, we need to remember some biblical guidance:

- "Am I now trying to win the approval of men, or of God? Or am I trying to please men? If I were still trying to please men, I would not be a servant of Christ" (Gal. 1:10).
- "On the contrary, we speak as men approved by God to be entrusted with the gospel. We are not trying to please men but God, who tests our hearts" (1 Thess. 2:4).

Second, when our decision might hurt others, we also need to ask, "Would I like to be treated like this?" This is another way to approach the Golden Rule, "Do to others as you would have them do to you" (Luke 6:31). We learned in chapter 3 that people naturally react when they believe someone is treating them unfairly. That's part of the moral law written upon human hearts. We further found that the moral law is not always apparent from our *actions*, but it is clearly revealed in our *reactions*.

So we should make a reality check of our fairness and ask how we would feel if situations were reversed. Notice we are not asking whether we *have* ever been treated as we plan to treat someone else.

One of the things that made Abraham Lincoln one of the most loved and most hated men in all of America at the same time was his issuing of the Emancipation Proclamation. It may surprise some to learn that Lincoln had great reservations about issuing the proclamation. It wasn't that he thought it was wrong, but rather, his reservations concerned the potential negative effects of issuing such a proclamation. As the McClellan campaign for Richmond failed, Lincoln decided to take the bold step of declaring that all slaves would be declared free. He called in his cabinet on July 22, 1862, and revealed to them his preliminary version of the Emancipation Proclamation. After the draft was read, Secretary of State Seward suggested that the proclamation be postponed until the Union had won a military victory to bolster it in the eyes of the nation. So Lincoln hesitated and put the proclamation aside and waited for things to get better. Unfortunately, defeat after defeat occurred, making things seem darker than ever.[14]

In August of 1862, Charles Sumner of Massachusetts wrote of Lincoln to John Bright in England: "He is hard to move. I urged him on the 4th of July to put forth an edict of emancipation, telling him he could make the day more sacred and historic than ever. He replied, 'I would do it if I were not afraid that half the officers would fling down their arms and three more States would rise.'"[15]

Finally, Lincoln could hesitate no longer. At a cabinet meeting on September 22, Lincoln read the proclamation again and stated his resolve to sign it on January 1, 1863. Cabinet member Montgomery Blair warned that this proclamation would send border states into the Southern fold and give Lincoln's foes in the North a club to use against him. But Lincoln would not be diverted. Two days later, on September 24, the preliminary Emancipation Proclamation was published for the country and the world to read. Concerning his hesitation, Lincoln said, "I can only trust God I have made no mistake. . . . It is now for the country and the world to pass judgment on it, and, may be, take action upon it."[16]

Lincoln had hesitations about issuing the Emancipation Proclamation, but he knew the cost of silence was too great. Sometimes we know what to do but are unsure of how to do it. We need to go to the next step for more guidance.

I—Identify the Greater Good

The fourth step in making a proper ethical decision is to identify the greater good. As we have seen, the Greater Good approach holds that there is a priority of values: God is more valued than persons, and persons are more valued than things. When there is an unavoidable conflict between ethical actions, the higher takes precedence over the lower. So, we should love God more than people, and we should love people more than things.

In this step, we must discover and obey the higher law that is applicable to our ethical dilemma.

- *Is it love for God over love for people?* Loving God is the greatest and highest commandment (Matt. 22:36–38). While we are commanded to love both God and man, our love for God must overrule our love for man. Loving God in this situation is to know the mind of God and obey it fully.
- *Is it love for people more than things?* We should never view the things of this world as treasures and treat people as toys (Matt. 22:39; 1 Tim. 6:17–19). First Timothy 6 tells us that God has given us things through our jobs to enjoy, but that we are to keep these things in proper perspective. Lying to people in business to gain things for ourselves or our company is wrong.
- *Is it loving others more than self?* While we can love ourselves, we are to love God first, then our neighbor, and finally ourselves (Luke 10:27). The Golden Rule sets a strong pattern to follow in most business decisions (Matt. 7:12). Asking, "How would I feel if I were in his shoes?" often makes the ethical choice clear.
- *Is it obeying God over human authority?* The principle behind Colossians 3:22 is that we should obey those in authority over us—the boss: "Slaves, obey your earthly masters in everything; and do it, not only when their eye is on you and to win their favor, but with sincerity of heart and reverence for the Lord."

Does this mean that we must obey our boss "in everything" and go along with an employer's wrong behavior? Verses 23–24 declare that our true boss is the Lord himself: "Whatever you do, work at it with all your heart, as working for the Lord, not for men, since you know that you will receive an inheritance from the Lord as a reward. It is the Lord Christ you are serving." When two bosses disagree with each other, the senior boss must be followed. Since the Lord is the "senior" boss, we must obey the Lord rather than our earthly boss when the two disagree.

So this fourth step is to discover what the overriding moral obligation is. Whenever possible, we are to look for a way to fulfill both obligations. "If it is possible, as far as it depends on you, live at peace with everyone" (Rom. 12:18). However, if two or more moral duties come into unavoidable conflict, we must follow the greater duty.

Lincoln identified the greater good in his decision to fight slavery. During the last week of December 1862, Congressman John Cavode found the president walking back and forth in his office with a troubled face. When he asked the president why he had to make the proclamation, the president replied, "I have studied that matter well; my mind is made up. . . . It must be done. I am driven to it. There is no other way out of our troubles. But although my duty is plain, it is in some respects painful, and I trust the people will understand that I act not in anger but in *expectation of a greater good.*"[17]

Lincoln broke down his "greater good" in a letter to the American people dated August 22, 1862:

> I would save the Union. I would save it in the shortest way under the Constitution. . . . My paramount object in this struggle is to save the Union, and is not either to save or to destroy slavery. If I could save the Union without freeing any slave, I would do it, and if I could save it by freeing all of the slaves, I would do it. . . . What I do about slavery, and the colored race, I do because I believe it helps to save the Union. . . . I have here stated my purpose according to my view of official duty; and I intend no modification of my oft-expressed personal wish that all men everywhere could be free.[18]

Lincoln's greater good held the Union as most important. Everything he did was to preserve it, including the difficult act of freeing the slaves. This does not mean that he felt slavery was tolerable, for he personally opposed it, rather that he understood his number one duty was to preserve the Union. His approach to others was that not only was slavery morally wrong, but it was dangerous to the Union. He stated to Congress, "In giving freedom to the slave, we assure freedom to the free—honorable alike in what we give, and what we preserve."[19]

Now we know *what* we should do, but *how* should we do it? Is there a way to please both God and the boss? The next step helps answer these questions.

C—Consider Consequences and Creative Alternatives

The fifth step in making a proper ethical decision is to consider two very important questions: What will be the consequences of your action, and are less costly creative alternatives available?

What are the consequences? As we saw in chapter 4, Christian ethics is duty-based (deontological) rather than ends-centered, whereby results decide (teleological). But this does not mean that the Christian does not consider the results. He or she simply does not use anticipated results to make up the rules. Nor does the ethical person use expected results as justification for violating rules. For he or she knows that a good does not justify evil means. Nonetheless, the ethical person does use good means (e.g., inoculation) to attain the best results. In fact, it is an important part of the decision-making process. As we note elsewhere, "This does not mean that consequences are not relevant for assessing the morality of an act. But consequences are not the only features in the matter, and when consequences are taken into account, they provide factual information for discovering what action is more in keeping with what is already our duty."[20]

Sometimes the right action can have difficult consequences. Once we know what God wants us to do, it would be wise to consider the consequences of our actions, if only to prepare ourselves or others for them. What will be the effects of this action on others and on me? What will be the possible short-term effects? What about the long-term effects?

This is a part of "counting the cost" (Luke 14:28). Other verses speak to this:

- "In his heart a man plans his course, but the LORD determines his steps" (Prov. 16:9).
- "The plans of the diligent lead to profit as surely as haste leads to poverty" (Prov. 21:5).

Lincoln understood the consequences of his actions. Speaking with two antislavery clergymen, he said, "We shall need all the anti-slavery feeling in this country, and more; you can go home and try to bring the people to your views; and you may say anything you like about me, if that will help. Don't spare me!" This he said with a laugh. Then gravely: "When the hour comes for dealing with slavery, I trust I will be willing to do my duty though it cost my life. And, gentlemen, lives will be lost."[21]

The Emancipation Proclamation was aimed at Europe as well as North and South America. England supported the South in order to keep its profitable cotton trade. Because of the war, nearly five hundred thousand were out of work in England. The London magazine *Punch* caricatured Lincoln with horns and a long tail. Henry Adams wrote that "England created a nightmare of its own and gave it the shape of Abraham Lincoln." Every problem England had at the time was blamed on Lincoln. Closer to home, the Richmond *Enquirer* fumed, "What shall we call him? Coward, assassin, savage, murderer of women and babies? Or shall we consider them all as embodied in the word fiend, and call him Lincoln, the Fiend?"[22]

Thinking through the possible consequences is a wise course of action and should not deter us from the right course of action but rather prepare us for the outcome. As there is a cost to every important decision, a wise person prepares for it.

Are creative alternatives available? In chapter 6 we will see how Daniel came up with a creative alternative to a wrong directive by his boss (Dan. 1:11–13). When facing an ethical dilemma in the workplace, see if you can come up with a creative option to wrong directives. We would be amazed at how open people are to creative alternatives if only we would come up with them. It takes a lot of thought, creativity, and prayer to come up with creative alternatives to ethical dilemmas, but they work. A way past a moral dilemma should always be sought. Only when the conflict is unavoidable should one set aside a lower moral principle to keep the higher one, for example, lying to save a life (Exod. 1:17–21).

To come up with a creative alternative, you must know three things:

1. *What is the goal?* What is the ultimate goal your boss wants to achieve? Some executives care only about the bottom-line profit. Knowing what the boss ultimately wants is the starting point for solving the problem.
2. *Is there a better way?* Is there a better way to accomplish the goal? Can you accomplish the same results using ethical methods? Daniel knew that his boss ultimately wanted physically healthy specimens and came up with an alternative that accomplished the goal (Daniel 1:10–21).
3. *Is there a wise approach?* How you present your position and creative alternative is very important. The "Oreo cookie method" is another Office Zoo taming tool one of the authors teaches that is effective for confronting a person or, in this case, sharing a differing position with your boss.[23] To present the creative alternative, sandwich the message between sweet cookies:

   - *Cookie.* Begin by saying something you respect or appreciate about your boss, or an area on which the two of you agree. Every person needs appreciation but not flattery. Most people see through flattery. You will certainly strike a responsive chord within a person that will break open the hard ground of his or her heart for your seed, the "cream."
   - *Cream.* Share your position on the issue. The cream of the cookie is the negative that must be communicated, whether it is a point of confrontation or a differing position.
   - *Cookie.* Finish by sharing positive intent that assumes the best about the person and gives the benefit of the doubt. This gives the person a good reputation to live up to and will encourage the person to consider your position.

Note the application of these principles in the following scenario.

Wendy, store manager for an office supply company, faces an ethical dilemma. Two weeks ago her boss called a meeting for today to discuss the loss of inventory in the store. Over the past two months, reams of paper, computer software, and even a leather chair have come up missing. No one can tell whether the theft came from store employees or warehouse employees.

Wendy trusts her employees but is less trusting of the warehouse staff. She has long suspected that Rody, the warehouse manager, and his employees have "sticky fingers," but until now the items missing have not been of much value.

Rob, the company owner, blew into Wendy's office with a beet-red face and a foul mouth. He threw onto her desk a list of missing items totaling over thirteen hundred dollars and demanded to know who is "robbing him blind." Wendy stammered that she did not know about the theft and could not identify a suspect without evidence.

Rob clenched his teeth and said, "We have to stop these thefts. You and Rody have two weeks to come up with a suspect. Otherwise, I will deduct the cost of the missing items from everyone's checks, store and warehouse employees alike."

Wendy countered, "But Rob, that's not fair to punish everyone for something that possibly only one person did. They are all going to be upset, and rightly so."

"Neither is it fair to expect me to absorb this loss," Rob countered, "and I am not going to do it. With my plan I get my money back, and I teach everyone a lesson. If you've got a better idea, then let's hear it. You've got two weeks."

Wendy has been trying to come up with ideas. While she has suspicions about two employees in the warehouse, she has no hard evidence that they are guilty. It would not be right to make someone the "sacrificial lamb," just to pacify Rob. Nor is it right for all the employees to be forced to pay for something they did not do. Her employees barely make enough as it is. To take money from them unfairly will destroy company morale.

Goal? Wendy knows she has to come up with a creative alternative to Rob's directive, so she starts with goals. Rob's goals are to stop the thefts, get his money back, and catch the thief. Getting the money back and catching the thief are impossible without evidence or a confession. So she focuses on the more realistic goal of instituting measures to prevent future thefts. This will not retrieve the money, but it will give Rob some peace of mind and put a system in place to prevent further thefts.

Better way? There has to be a better way to stop the thefts than requiring all the workers to pay for something they did not do. So Wendy develops a security system recommendation that includes video cameras in the store, the warehouse, and the employee parking lot. Presently, there is no security system at all, so this would send a message to everyone.

Wise approach? At her meeting with Rob, Wendy uses the Oreo cookie method to present her creative alternative. She starts with the cookie, telling Rob how she respects him for building a good company from scratch. One of his mottos of success is to give everyone a "fair deal." His fairness is something she has always appreciated about him, and salespeople brag to customers that they can trust this store to be fair. She moves into the cream part. Accusing someone without proof or making everyone pay for one person's theft will not be giving his employees a "fair deal." His reputation will be destroyed.

Unfortunately there is no way to retrieve the stolen money, but there is a way to prevent it from happening again. If he is interested, she has a proposal for a security system that is effective and affordable. She concludes with the other cookie: she knows that he wants to do the right thing, and she is ready to help him do that.

Rob looks down at his papers, then says, "Okay, Wendy. Let's hear your security proposal."

Lincoln was also a person who liked to come up with creative alternatives. He passionately pursued two creative alternatives to going to war over the slavery issue. One was the colonization of black people who were to be freed. The president asked for, and Congress passed, an act recognizing the black republics of Haiti and Liberia. Free blacks were not enthusiastic about this proposal.

Lincoln also suggested "gradual compensated abolishment," a plan he presented to Congress in March 1862. In July of that year, Lincoln met with congressmen from the states remaining in the Union that recognized slavery—Missouri, Kentucky, Maryland, and Delaware. He pleaded the case for this gradual, compensated abolishment of slavery, starting in their states.

Lincoln said, "I assure you that in my opinion, if you had all voted for the resolution . . . of last March, the war would now be substantially ended." He believed that, with the slaves freed by purchase in the border states, the states that had seceded would see that they could not long keep up the war. The money spent for buying slaves and setting them free would shorten the war. "How much better to thus save the money which else we sink forever in the war?"

But the border state men privately rejected his plan, and nothing came of Lincoln's plan to buy the slaves and set them free.[24]

S—Stand for God

The final step in making a proper ethical decision is to decide to stand for God no matter what. Sometimes you can get your boss to change his or her mind as Daniel did (Daniel 1). But at other times this will not work, as in the case of Daniel's three friends (Daniel 3) and then Daniel himself (Daniel 6). What do you do then?

To stand for God you must make two decisions:

1. *Purpose in your heart that you will stand for God no matter what.* You must make a commitment to stand for God before you are faced with an ethical dilemma:

   - "But Daniel resolved not to defile himself with the royal food and wine, and he asked the chief official for permission not to defile himself this way" (Dan. 1:8). Daniel made up his mind. He set it upon his heart. He made a conscious, deliberate choice that he would not defile himself with the king's food.
   - "Therefore, my dear brothers, stand firm. Let nothing move you. Always give yourselves fully to the work of the Lord, because you know that your labor in the Lord is not in vain" (1 Cor. 15:58).
   - "Be on your guard; stand firm in the faith; be men of courage; be strong" (1 Cor. 16:13).
   - "Therefore put on the full armor of God, so that when the day of evil comes, you may be able to stand your ground, and after you have done everything, to stand. Stand firm then, with the belt of truth buckled around your waist, with the breastplate of righteousness in place" (Eph. 6:13–14).
   - Tertullian, a second-century church father, spoke to the need of being willing to stand for God no matter what. Some of the Christians were making idols as their profession, and Tertullian confronted them, saying that this

was wrong. A Christian idol-maker came to Tertullian privately, seeking some sort of compromise. After he explained his difficulty, he exclaimed, "What can I do? I must live!" Tertullian replied, "Must you?"[25]

2. *Remember that suffering leads to glory.* The Lord promises that suffering for doing right will one day lead to glory with God. Notice that the Lord does not promise that everything will work out at work, that your boss will love you, or that you will not lose your job. But he does promise that you will receive glory from him in the proper time.

- "In this you greatly rejoice, though now for a little while you may have had to suffer grief in all kinds of trials. These have come so that your faith—of greater worth than gold, which perishes even though refined by fire—may be proved genuine and may result in praise, glory and honor when Jesus Christ is revealed" (1 Peter 1:6–7).
- "But rejoice that you participate in the sufferings of Christ, so that you may be overjoyed when his glory is revealed" (1 Peter 4:13; cf. 2 Cor. 4:17).
- "So then, those who suffer according to God's will should commit themselves to their faithful Creator and continue to do good" (1 Peter 4:19).

Notice some thoughts from 1 Peter 4:19. Suffering may be God's will for our lives. That may not sound very exciting, except when we realize that God controls how much and how long we suffer. Next, when suffering comes, we should commit ourselves to God. The word translated "commit" here means to entrust

The ETHICS Compass

E—Examine the Facts

- Get all of the facts and examine them carefully.
- Use the rephrasing tool to make sure you have the correct facts.

T—(Seek the) Truth

- Seek wisdom from the Bible.
- Pray to God for wisdom, and he will answer this prayer.

H—Hesitate

- Ask yourself, "Why are you hesitating?"
- Ask yourself, "Would I want to be treated like this?"

I—Identify the Greater Good

- Is it love for God over love for man (Matt. 22:36-38)?
- Is it love for people more than things (Matt. 22:39; 1 Tim. 6:17–19)?
- Is it loving others more than self (Luke 10:27)?
- Is it obeying God over authority (Col. 3:22–24)?
- Is it fear of God over fear of man (Prov. 1:7; 29:25)?

C—Consider Consequences and Creative Alternatives

- What will be the consequences?
- Are there any creative alternatives available?
- Use the Oreo cookie method to share your ethical position.

S—Stand for God

- Purpose in your heart that you will stand for God no matter what.
- Remember that suffering leads to glory.

something valuable to another. We place our lives and our future in God's hands. Finally, we should continue to do good. That is, we are to live ethically in an ethical wilderness.

Lincoln understood that the "fiery trial" he and the nation faced was from God. How they stood through it would be remembered by all. In his address to Congress on December 1, 1862, Lincoln wrote, "Fellow-citizens, we cannot escape history. We of this Congress and this administration, will be remembered in spite of ourselves. No personal significance or insignificance can spare one or another of us. The fiery trial through which we pass, will light us down, in honor or dishonor, to the latest generation."[26]

On New Year's Day, 1863, Lincoln was to sign the Emancipation Proclamation. That morning there was a huge celebration at the White House, and Lincoln spent three hours shaking hands and greeting visitors. That afternoon Secretary Seward walked over to the White House, ready for Lincoln to put his signature on the document to make it official. Before signing, Lincoln said: "I never, in my life, felt more certain that I was doing right, than I do in signing this paper. But I have been receiving calls and shaking hands since nine o'clock this morning, till my arm is stiff and numb. Now this signature is one that will be closely examined, and if they find my hand trembled they will say, 'he had some compunctions.' But anyway, it is going to be done." And with that, he slowly and carefully signed his full name—"Abraham Lincoln"—something he rarely did.[27]

While we may not like it, standing for God usually leads to suffering at work, at home, at school, and in all of life. When trouble occurs, we need to remember an old story:

> Two travelers were setting up camp for the night. The one said to the other, "Remember not to put the stakes in too deeply. We're leaving in the morning."

As Christians, we are but travelers in this world. As the traditional Southern gospel song testifies, "This world is not my home." While we may suffer, it is only for a short time.

Conclusion

The ETHICS Compass is a step-by-step guide to making ethical decisions. The ETHICS Compass follows through proper ethical concepts that are necessary to consider in making the right, ethical decision.

The next three chapters will apply the ETHICS Compass to Daniel and his workplace. Daniel and his friends faced the ethical dilemma of a society in which people did whatever it took to get ahead. They kissed up to the boss and went with the flow. Daniel and his friends, however, made the proper decisions when facing their ethical dilemmas.

Ethical Dilemmas in Daniel's Workplace

6

Between a Rock and a Hard Place

Peter is a salesman for Visser Steel, a large stainless steel coil distributor in the Midwest. Walter has represented the company in the largest sales territory, but he will soon retire. Peter is to take over this territory and first wants to meet its clients. Walter sits down with Peter to give him an overview of his new clients before his tour.

"Pete, we need to discuss Johnson Ruler before you leave. Old Johnson of Johnson Ruler has some idiosyncrasies, and he has made demands of me that you will find somewhat uncomfortable," Walter says slowly.

"Such as . . . ?" Peter asks.

"Well, I only bring this up because I know you're a religious man. Johnson will only discuss our business deals at a local strip club. I never really liked it, but he is our biggest client. To lose him would be devastating to Visser Steel."

Peter is a Christian, and he has tried to maintain a strong witness at work. He keeps his Bible on his desk and speaks about his faith openly. Now he faces a huge ethical dilemma. He will not go to such a place. On the other hand, he can't risk losing such a big client. He is truly "between a rock and a hard place."

In the Bible's book of Daniel, chapter 1, we meet a worker with a similar problem. Daniel, though born of noble birth, has been taken captive and placed in a volatile work environment in the foreign land of Babylon. Daniel and his three friends are being forced to do things the king's way—or else. To do what their boss demands will result in violating their moral standards. To refuse to do so will likely result in immediate termination (literally).

How Did Daniel Get in This Tight Spot?

Since the story of Daniel is the central case study for chapters 6–8 of this book, we will look at how Daniel came to be in his difficult situation.

In 605 BC, the two superpowers of the world, Egypt and Babylon, were battling for control of that part of the world. At the Battle of Carchemish, Nebuchadnezzar, the crown prince of Babylon, nearly annihilated the Egyptian army and won dominance of the known world. The Egyptians were forced to retreat south to their home, which opened Palestine to the control of the Babylonians. Soon Nebuchadnezzar's hand grasped Jerusalem, forcing Jehoiakim, the king of Judah, to submit to him. Later that year, Nebuchadnezzar returned to Babylon and was crowned king, bringing captured goods and captives with him, fulfilling the prophecy of Isaiah 39:6–7.

One of these captives was Daniel, who was taken from his family and delivered to Babylon. Daniel, along with a number of other Hebrew teens, was part of the first wave of captives brought hostage to Babylon. Daniel was ripped from his homeland, his family, and his friends, and he probably never returned to his home again. Nebuchadnezzar was the king under whom Daniel served in chapters 1–4.

A New Job and a New Dilemma

Job openings. As the new king, Nebuchadnezzar wanted "fresh blood" in his administration. Like any new boss, he wanted to select his own staff. He looked for people with great potential, enthusiasm, and a different perspective than the counselors of his late father. Since he was leader of the known world, he needed advisors from various parts of his empire to help him govern wisely.

Job interviews. Who better to fill the bill than some of the new captives he had personally been impressed with and selected to bring back with him? Nebuchadnezzar had specific criteria for evaluating the candidates (Dan. 1:4):

- *Malleability.* They had to be "young men." The Hebrew word translated "youths" refers to teenagers, probably between the ages of thirteen and fifteen. Young people are less myopic and ingrained in traditional ways of doing things. Also, young people are more malleable, so the king could shape them into the kind of servants he wanted.
- *Fitness.* They had to be without "defect." No physical or mental imperfections would keep them from fulfilling their job requirements.
- *A professional appearance.* They had to be "handsome" or "good-looking" (NASB). They were attractive or knew how to look their best. The king wanted the best-looking people to stand before him and to represent him.
- *Education.* They were to be "well informed." Hebrew youths of that age would have already acquired an extensive education. They were to be able

to pass aptitude tests as well as be quick learners since they would have to learn a new language and customs to serve their new boss.

- *Social skills.* They had to be qualified or have the "ability" (NASB) to serve in the king's palace. Nebuchadnezzar was concerned about their social skills as well as their physical and mental abilities. They had to display the poise, manners, and social graces necessary to work in the palace.

On-the-Job Training

Daniel and his friends were the "cream of the crop" in Judea (Dan. 1:6), so Nebuchadnezzar introduced these young men and others to a carefully planned course of education. The project manager for this training project was Ashpenaz, who was to select the finest and most qualified candidates. After three years' training, they would be presented to Nebuchadnezzar for service. The training process involved job adjustment, a new identity, education, and diet.

- *Job.* The Hebrew captives were to join Babylon's government, which had kidnapped them and also desecrated the temple in Jerusalem. They were now to serve the very monster that had changed their lives (Dan. 1:5).
- *Identity.* Daniel and his friends were given Babylonian names (Dan. 1:7). No doubt the Hebrew names of Daniel and his friends may have been offensive to the king. Their Hebrew names pointed to the God of Israel while their Babylonian names would now point to the heathen gods of Babylon.
- *Education.* The Hebrew captives had already completed most of their education, as Daniel demonstrated by his moral stance in Daniel 1:8. The additional education probably involved learning Aramaic, which the Hebrews needed to learn to serve effectively. It was the language of the land (v. 4).
- *Diet.* Daniel and his friends were to eat from the king's table. This honor meant that they could eat the finest food available. Their menu was not the "bread and water" a captive would normally eat. Rather, they had the opportunity to eat gourmet food at every meal (Dan. 1:5).[1]

Curiously, Daniel was bothered by only one aspect of his training. He objected to his new diet, saying that eating food served at the king's table would "defile" him (Dan. 1:8). Why was this new diet an ethical dilemma for Daniel but the other three new aspects were not?

- *Job.* By serving Nebuchadnezzar, Daniel and his friends were actually enabling the Babylonian government to continue its evil work around the world. They could have felt unpatriotic or even been thought of as traitors. But Daniel had no difficulty in serving a government that had defeated his nation and defiled the temple. There were possibly three reasons for this.

First, Judah had sinned and its judgment was prophesied and fulfilled by God. Nebuchadnezzar was but a tool (Jeremiah 7). Second, to seek the good of Babylon was to obey God. The exiles were to "seek the welfare of the city where I have sent you into exile" (Jer. 29:7). Third, in government positions they could have extraordinary influence for God by being a part of this government as Joseph had in Egypt, generations earlier.

- *Identity.* Every time someone called Daniel or one of his three friends by his new name, that person was blessing a pagan god. If anything might defile a person, surely being given a new name that praised a pagan deity would be at the top of the list! But it did not seem to bother Daniel. First, they had no choice in the names that were given, for the king could call them whatever he wanted. Second, Daniel was aware that Joseph was given his name by Pharaoh without any hint that God considered the name defiling. Third, to change another's name was to claim authority over that person, but Daniel knew that God was still in control, not the king, as later events in the book of Daniel reveal.

- *Education.* Why would Daniel not have opposed an attempt by Nebuchadnezzar to brainwash the Hebrew captives to renounce their God? Could it be that this new education was more for the purpose of training in the Babylonian language and business practices? They undoubtedly heard polytheistic theology, but a pagan school did not seem to be a defilement. These captives were not impressionable children who would swallow everything they were taught. They were grounded in the Scripture to know such things as what would defile them (Dan. 1:8). They knew that both Joseph and Moses had been raised and educated in a foreign land, without condemnation from God.

- *Diet.* For some reason, the only thing Daniel considered defiling was a Babylonian steak! Daniel probably had two reasons for concern. First, the king would serve food considered unclean by the law of Moses (Lev. 11:45–47; Deut. 14:3–21). Second, the food and wine served at the king's table probably came from the temple, where it had been offered in worship to heathen gods (Exod. 34:15; Num. 25:1–2; Deut. 32:37–38).

The real issue was this: in the Babylonian way of thinking, to eat the food that was offered to their idols was, in essence, to worship these idols. So if the Jewish captives were to eat this food, it would be a public statement that they had forsaken God for the worship of idols.[2] That was where Daniel drew the line and said, "No further." The ethical dilemma was this: for Daniel and his young friends to get ahead, they would have to violate their moral standards and do so at a public table in the view of all. This they would not do.

Daniel here seems to be informing us that we must choose our battles wisely. When you are hired by a company, you have a *new job*. Unless you work for a Christian ministry, you will be working for Babylon. You likely will have a pagan boss, ungodly co-workers, and a bottom line of profit as all that matters. With the emphasis in business on growing bigger and more profitable, ethical dilemmas abound.

Certainly working for Babylon has its challenges, like being surrounded by ungodly people who have ungodly purposes. Your boss and co-workers may use language or make comments that you find offensive. As we showed in our book *Bringing Your Faith to Work*, these challenges are opportunities for witnessing more than obstacles to working.[3] Working for a secular company does not mean that you are not working for God. In *Bringing Your Faith to Work*, we learned that God works, so work has dignity. It is good as it meets others' needs and a gift from God as it brings satisfaction. When we work, we are co-workers with God.[4]

With each new job, you will also receive a *new identity*. That does not mean the company will now change your name, but that your world is now wrapped up in your job. You are a part of your job, and your job is a part of you. The company's schedule becomes your schedule. While this is normal, one must take care not to let work demands exceed the boundaries needed for family and faith.

You will also receive a *new education*. You will receive training to become proficient in your line of work. No doubt you will hear things that you will not agree with, such as hedonistic philosophy and different worldviews, value systems, and approaches to ethics. When presented with such information, you should approach it as you would approach dining on a fish: eat the meat and leave the bones.

But when your new job requires that you partake of a *new diet*, watch out! The ethical dilemma for Daniel and his young friends was that they would violate their moral standards in the view of all. When the first plate of Babylonian filet mignon with steak fries was placed in front of Daniel and his three friends, everyone at the table stopped eating to see what they would do. The other Jewish exiles in this program had accepted the new diet and eaten their fill of steak and fries (Dan. 1:13, 15). But for Daniel and his friends to take the first bite would not only defile them in the eyes of God, it would defile them in the eyes of others. They faced an ethical dilemma, being far from home, with intense pressure to conform, and compromisers all around them.

When your job requires that you violate moral or ethical standards, you need to push the plate away and stand up from the king's table. To compromise your stand, even for only one time, will defile you in the eyes of God, yourself, and those around you who are watching.

But knowing all this does not resolve the question of how to stay undefiled and still keep your job.

Using the ETHICS Compass

Daniel and his three friends were forced to go the king's way or else. To accept the king's food would mean to violate their ethical standards set by God. To refuse would mean instant death. Yet Daniel found a way to please his boss and God. Let's apply the ETHICS Compass to learn how Daniel solved this ethical dilemma.

Examine the Facts

The first step in making a proper ethical decision is to make sure you have all the facts before you and then examine them carefully. Daniel learned of the king's requirements for the Jewish exiles, which included being given food and drink from the king's table for a period of three years (Dan. 1:5). Daniel also found out that the goal of this menu was to present the best-looking candidates to the king for selection (v. 10).

Let's go back and visit Peter in his dilemma. When Peter heard about the customer's demand for business meetings in a strip club, he was speechless for a minute. Then he spent the next thirty minutes asking Walter all kinds of questions about his arrangement with old Johnson. He needed information! When did this arrangement begin? How did it begin? What was Visser Steel's sales history with Johnson Ruler? How can one possibly conduct business at a strip club? How did Walter know that Johnson would consider no other alternatives? What suggestions did he have?

Seek the Truth

The second step in making a proper ethical decision is to seek what God has to say about this matter. What does the Bible have to say about the issue being faced? Is it a black-and-white or more of a gray issue according to the Bible?

Daniel knew that the truth included the following:

- To eat the king's food would defile him in God's eyes (Dan. 1:8).
- This food was probably unclean according to the law of Moses (Deut. 14:3–21; Lev. 11:45–47).
- Food and wine served at Nebuchadnezzar's table was probably associated with the worship of heathen gods (Exod. 34:15; Num. 25:1–2; Deut. 32:37–38).

Peter's ethical dilemma was that he was expected to conduct business in an improper environment—a strip club! As he examined the Bible, he came across some pivotal verses:

- "Keep . . . from the immoral woman, from the smooth tongue of the wayward wife. Do not lust in your heart after her beauty or let her captivate you with her eyes, for the prostitute reduces you to a loaf of bread, and the adulteress preys upon your very life" (Prov. 6:24–26).
- "You have heard that it was said, 'Do not commit adultery.' But I tell you that anyone who looks at a woman lustfully has already committed adultery with her in his heart" (Matt. 5:27–28).
- "It is God's will that you should be sanctified: that you should avoid sexual immorality; that each of you should learn to control his own body in a way that is holy and honorable, not in passionate lust like the heathen, who do not know God" (1 Thess. 4:3–5).
- "I made a covenant with my eyes not to look lustfully at a girl" (Job 31:1).

Peter's ethical dilemma was a black-and-white decision. He knew that conducting business in a strip club would violate his conscience and his witness and compromise his moral integrity. Since his decision was clearly spelled out by the Bible, what should he do next?

Hesitate

This third step in making a proper ethical decision is to see if there is anything about our decision that makes us hesitate before proceeding. Do we sense a "red flag" or a "little voice" whispering to slow down or stop altogether? Ask, "Am I hesitating because I know what the Bible says to do, but I don't know how to do it? Or am I hesitating because I know what the Bible says to do, but I am afraid to do it?"

Daniel certainly could have had some hesitations about refusing to go along with his new diet:

- He had no choice in the matter as the diet was assigned by the king (Dan. 1:5, 10).
- To refuse the king would mean certain death (Dan. 1:10).
- The other Jewish exiles had gone ahead and compromised (Dan. 1:13, 15).

Peter knew that the Bible said he must keep himself pure and avoid sexual immorality. Thus he could not go to a strip club, but his hesitation was that he was unsure how to proceed. He needed to go to the next step for more guidance.

Identify the Greater Good

The fourth step in making a proper ethical decision is to identify the greater good. The Greater Good approach holds that there is a priority of values that places God over other persons and persons over things. Whenever there is a conflict between two of these, the higher takes precedence over the lower. For example, we should love God more than people, and we should love people over things.

Daniel had to discover and obey the higher law that was applicable to his ethical dilemma:

- *Is it love for God over love for man?* Loving God was the greatest and highest commandment for Daniel (Deut. 6:5–6).
- *Is it love for people more than things?* This was not applicable to Daniel's specific dilemma in chapter 1.
- *Is it loving others more than self?* Truly Daniel was to love others, including the king, more than himself (Lev. 19:18). However, he must love God over others.
- *Is it obeying God over authority?* Like the midwives of old, Daniel had to fear God more than he feared the king (Exod. 1:17).

Peter must discover and obey the higher law that is applicable to his ethical dilemma:

- *Is it love for God over love for man?* Peter was to love God more than man, including himself. His fear of losing a valuable client could cause him to love himself and go along with the strip club business office.
- *Is it love for people more than things?* Peter's love for his wife was more important than his job and the things it provided.
- *Is it loving others more than self?* Once again, Peter was to love his wife more than himself.
- *Is it obeying God over authority?* As Peter prepared to leave his office and fly out to meet with Mr. Johnson, Mr. Visser came up to Peter and said, "Well, Peter, we're counting on you to do whatever it takes to keep the Johnson Ruler account. No matter how unpleasant it may seem to you. I want it to be very obvious to you that this account is extremely important to me." While Mr. Visser did not come out and explicitly command Peter to go to the strip bar, he made it obvious that his job was dependent on successfully retaining this account. While Peter was to obey his earthly boss, he knew that he must truly obey his heavenly boss in this situation.

So Peter knew what he should do, considering that he could not in good conscience go to a strip club to conduct business. But was there a way to obey God *and* man? The next step gives Peter the necessary guidance he was seeking.

Consider Consequences and Creative Alternatives

The fifth step in making a proper ethical decision is to consider the consequences of your action and whether any creative alternatives are available.

Daniel knew there would be consequences to his decision, for himself, for his three friends, and even for his immediate supervisor (Dan. 1:10). Ashpenaz was not being dramatic when he said that he would lose his head. In this workplace, one could lose life as well as position.

When facing his ethical dilemma in the workplace, could Daniel come up with a creative option to wrong directives? To do so, Daniel needed to know three things:

1. *What was the ultimate goal of Daniel's boss?* It was to have the healthiest people possible working for him.
2. *What might be a better way to accomplish the goal?* Once Daniel knew what his boss ultimately wanted (physically healthy specimens), he came up with an ethically pleasing alternative that accomplished his boss's goal.
3. How should he present the matter? Remember the Oreo cookie approach from chapter 5? Notice how carefully and wisely Daniel approached his superiors:

   - *Proper channels.* He went to the right person, the one who would have the right to make the decision and also would bear the responsibility for it (Dan. 1:8).
   - *Respect.* He asked for permission (v. 8). He did not demand or stage a strike. He showed respect for authority—even ungodly authority. Notice in verse 12, he said, "Please" and "let us." Usually, when we respond with respect and a recognition of our authority's position, they are more open to us.
   - *Creative alternative.* Daniel's creative alternative (vv. 11–13) was a reasonable test (only vegetables and water) that was time limited (ten days) and measurable ("compare our appearance"). Often authorities care only about the "bottom line," and any way that accomplishes it is fine with them. Nebuchadnezzar wasn't sitting on his throne thinking, "How can I make the Jewish captives' lives more miserable? I know! I'll make them eat my gourmet food." No, he only wanted the best and healthiest people working for him.
   - *Final decision.* The supervisor was to make the comparison and the final call (v. 13). Few authorities argue with having the final say on a new initiative or approach.

Like Daniel, Peter needed to consider these two very important questions: What will be the consequences of my actions, and are any creative alternatives available?

If Peter goes to the strip bar and conducts business, he may keep the account. But there is no guarantee of that. We are tempted to believe that if we compromise our stand and go along with the crowd, we will be accepted and successful. But even if Peter did compromise, Johnson could reject him and drop the account. Then what would Peter have gained? He would have gained nothing while losing much. If Peter does what he feels pressured to do, he will lose his clear conscience with God, his wife, and himself. Not only that, but Peter will also lose his witness on the job, which he has worked hard to build. Peter's upcoming trip is the buzz of the workplace. Peter even hears that there is a betting pool as to whether he will go to the strip bar.

On the other hand, if Peter does not go to the strip bar and loses the Johnson Ruler account, this will be a blow to Visser Steel and will probably cost him his job.

Can Peter come up with a creative option to a wrong situation? If Daniel, a teenager of fifteen, could come up with a creative alternative to his ethical dilemma, so can Peter. To do this Peter needs to know three things:

1. *The goal.* The goal is to keep the Johnson Ruler account.
2. *The better way.* Can Peter accomplish the same results using an ethical approach? After praying about it, Peter calls Mr. Johnson to say that he and his wife, Marilyn, are going to be in the Johnsons' town. They would love to take him and Mrs. Johnson out to dinner. Surprised by the invitation, Mr. Johnson says that his wife always loves going out to eat. Peter and his wife fly out (Marilyn at Peter's expense) and take Mr. and Mrs. Johnson to a nice restaurant. The women hit it off, and Peter discusses a couple of sales proposals.
3. *The wise approach.* Johnson leans over and says with a wink, "Pete, I usually like to discuss our business in another environment." Peter leans over as well and whispers, "Mr. Johnson, you're a successful businessman. A successful businessman never takes his best people for granted [with this, Peter nods at Johnson's wife]. I think that this is a healthier business environment for both of us. You're a wise man. I'm sure you'll agree." Johnson sits back with a frown, but then his wife asks him to tell one of his funny stories, which Johnson thoroughly loves to do. On the way out of the restaurant, Johnson pulls Peter aside and says, "You know, once I figured out what you were doing, I was ticked off. But now, I've got to admit: no sleazy strip club, a good dinner, the wives hit it off, and we all had some good laughs. I think I actually like doing business this way. Let's do it again next quarter!" Peter smiles and agrees. He can't wait to get back to the office and tell them about his creative alternative.

Stand for God

The final step in making a proper ethical decision is to decide to stand for God no matter what, even if it hurts your career or purse (Ps. 15:4). To stand for God you must make two decisions. First, purpose in your heart that you will stand for God no matter what. Daniel had made up his mind to stand for God (Dan. 1:8). If his creative alternative was not allowed, Daniel would have suffered for God. Daniel had resolved not to defile himself. He had made a conscious, deliberate choice: he was not going to defile himself by eating the king's gourmet menu of unclean food.

Peter made the same decision as Daniel. He would stand for God no matter what. He thought his creative alternative would work. It might also anger his client and cost his job.

Second, remember that suffering leads to glory. How did Daniel and his three friends suffer in Daniel 1? Consider that for three years their diet consisted of nothing but water and vegetables when they could have been enjoying the food the king enjoyed. To any meat-and-potatoes person, that would constitute suffering. The glory came at the end of three years when the king selected all four to serve in his palace. As the king interviewed them, he found that there were none to equal them (v. 19). In fact, the king found them to be ten times wiser than anyone currently serving him (v. 20).

Peter did not suffer, but his obedience led to glory, both now and forever. Paul said, "For our light and momentary troubles are achieving for us an eternal glory that far outweighs them all" (2 Cor. 4:17).

Conclusion

In Daniel 1, Daniel and his three friends were placed between an ethical "rock and a hard place," forced to go the king's way or else. To obey their boss would violate their moral standards. But to refuse to obey the king would mean certain death. They faced the dilemma of how to please God *and* people. Fortunately, they were able to please both. Sometimes that isn't possible. In the next chapter, on Daniel chapter 3, the issue is what to do when one must choose whether to please God *or* people.

7

Kissing Up to the Boss

Rick is a salesman for a large computer software company that has fallen on hard times. To make the company more profitable, they brought in a new head of sales, Jean. She has a reputation for being tough and demanding absolute loyalty from her staff. On her first day, Jean calls a meeting of her new sales staff to introduce herself, her expectations, and her plans. Jean tells about companies she has turned around. The way she tells it, her results are impressive. From now on, there will be one way to sell products—her way. Anyone who doesn't will be history. As she talks, Rick muses that Jean reminds him of Cruella De Vil, the villainess in the Walt Disney cartoon *101 Dalmatians*.

Jean unveils one of her plans. "We need to clear out current inventory and make room for new software. All of you have to make it your top priority to move this old software off the shelves or else."

An uncomfortable silence hangs in the air. Finally, John responds. "Jean, we've tried to move that software, but no one is interested in those products. What's your plan?"

"I'm glad you asked," Jean smiled. "You're going to love this. We will market our current software as new software—an upgrade over what our main competitor now offers. You will inform current and potential clients that the software they currently own is obsolete. We have the software they need to remain competitive."

"But what about the new software that is supposed to come out next spring? What do we do then?" Kelly asked.

"We'll simply go back to our clients next spring and tell them that their software once again is obsolete and they need our new software. Think about it—we'll clear out the old inventory and make money, then turn around and sell the real new software and make more money. When your clients complain next spring, simply blame it on the competition, which keeps developing new software to gain a competitive edge. It's foolproof!" Jean exclaims with a smirk.

Rick, the lone Christian in the sales department, has strong misgivings about Jean's deceptive approach. He raises his hand.

"Yes, Rick."

Rick decides to approach the issue by using the rephrasing tool. He carefully repeats what Jean has said: "Jean, let me make sure I understand you. Our company is now to market our older software as a new upgrade over our competitors and selling it at higher prices. And as long as we make money, you are okay with that. Is that correct?"

Jean narrows her eyes and says, "Yep."

"But it's not true. Our software is not new, and their software is not obsolete."

Jean laughs. "All software will eventually become obsolete. We're telling the truth . . . sort of. And we all will make a lot of money doing it!"

Rick shakes his head. "Jean, I have spent years building a trust relationship with my clients. They don't have a lot of computer savvy, which is why they buy from me. They trust and respect me. I can't look them in the face and lie to them."

Jean points her finger at Rick. "Get on board or you're out!"

Rick says nothing else and looks down. After all, he has his family and new home to think about.

"Anyone else have any comments?" Jean says with arms crossed and eyebrows raised. The sales staff suddenly bubbles with enthusiasm.

"I think it's great!"

"We're glad you're here, Jean!"

"We're on board with you, Jean!"

Everyone praises Jean except Rick. As a Christian, Rick faces an ethical dilemma of whether to please God or his boss. He feels that he has to "kiss up to the boss" or else. What does he do?

You Think Your Boss Is Tough to Work For!

A 2001 survey by Progressive Insurance found that most automobile accidents happen close to home.[1] They found that 52 percent of accidents happen within five miles of home. An astonishing 77 percent happen within fifteen miles of home. Beside the fact we spend most of our time there, another reason for this statistic could be that we can get so used to familiar roads that we pay less attention to them than to roads with which we are unfamiliar.

Those who have been around the Bible for a long time may approach familiar accounts in much the same way—that is, we pay less attention to them than to parts with which we are less familiar. The story of Shadrach, Meshach, and Abednego and the fiery furnace is such a story because many of us learned it as children.

When we approach Daniel 3 from a new perspective—as the account of three workers who felt they had to "kiss up to the boss" or else—the story comes alive. We must approach this story from the workplace perspective because that is exactly its setting. We have an egomaniac boss, an ethical dilemma, ingratiating co-workers, uncompromising examples, company snitches, and a hot finish.

- *Egomaniac boss.* We met Nebuchadnezzar, the absolute ruler of the known world, earlier. By the time covered in Daniel 3, he had become an egomaniac. As the British historian Lord Acton said in 1887, "Power tends to corrupt; absolute power corrupts absolutely."[2]
- *Ethical dilemma.* What did this self-absorbed boss decide to do? What was the ethical dilemma? He decided to build an image of himself ninety feet high and nine feet wide (Dan. 3:1), probably constructed of wood overlaid with gold. He commanded that his staff in particular and the nation generally must bow before and worship this eight-story statue (vv. 2–7). This was not to be simply an act of respect. The word *worship* is found in this chapter ten times. Why would he do such a thing? He probably wanted to ensure loyalty among his staff and eliminate potential factions caused by the differing religions represented among his servants. Ultimately, he also wanted to glorify himself. Anyone who did not bow down to the image would be thrown into the fiery furnace. If you ever thought you had it bad by being forced to kiss up to the boss, you should have tried working at Nebuchadnezzar's office!

To operate with an effective workplace, leaders need loyalty and obedience from staff. But when their demands are bent on glorifying themselves with no recourse, no good will come. Godly employees must always be alert to the actions of their superiors, as we shall discuss in chapter 11.

- *Ingratiating co-workers.* Among Nebuchadnezzar's office staff, who oversaw his affairs and administered his realm, most had no trouble bowing down to the boss. Those listed as assembled for the dedication of the image included satraps (regional governors), prefects (lieutenant governors), governors (administrators of territories), advisers, treasurers, judges, magistrates, and provincial officials (Dan. 3:3). These government leaders knew that they had to do what their boss wanted or suffer the consequences. Those present included captive Jews (1:3–4, 13, 15) who bowed down and kissed up with everyone else. In every workplace ingratiating co-workers can be seen kissing up to the boss. They laugh at his jokes, praise her plans or marketing strategy, and never, ever disagree or disobey. If it takes bowing down before an idol to get ahead, they are on their knees.

- *Uncompromising examples.* In the midst of this workplace worship, three leaders refused to kiss up to the boss. We first met Shadrach, Meshach, and Abednego in Daniel 1:7. Because of their excellent interview with Nebuchadnezzar, they were given positions in his service. Only these three refused to bow down and worship the golden idol (Dan. 3:8–12).

What do we know about these three men? First, they were excellent employees. We know this because some years have passed since Daniel 1, and they have been promoted to very high positions in the government (2:49). "But there are some Jews whom you have set over the affairs of the province of Babylon—Shadrach, Meshach and Abednego—who pay no attention to you, O king. They neither serve your gods nor worship the image of gold you have set up" (3:12).

Second, we know that they were respectful to their boss, despite the accusations of those who denounced them. Knowing what awaited them, they attended the ceremony anyway. They may have expected never to leave alive.

Conspicuously absent in this story is Daniel, who is thought to have written the book that bears his name. He does not include anything about himself here. The best guess is that, since he had been promoted to a high position like that of a prime minister (Dan. 2:48), he may have been out of the country on business. If Daniel had been present, we can be certain that he would not have bowed down either (see Daniel 6).[3]

- *Company snitches.* In every company some employees snitch on anyone who does not follow every rule or policy. When everyone else had their forehead to the ground before the idol, the three Jews stood. Quickly the company snitches found the king and reported (Dan. 3:8–12). Notice that their motivation is based on jealousy. Look carefully at 3:12 again: "But there are some Jews whom you have set over the affairs of the province of Babylon—Shadrach, Meshach and Abednego—who pay no attention to you, O king. They neither serve your gods nor worship the image of gold you have set up." These "astrologers" (NIV) who made the accusations were Chaldeans (NASB), natives of Babylon who considered Daniel and his three friends to be outsiders and foreigners. They never got over their jealousy of these foreigners being promoted to positions over them.

When Faced with Kissing Up to the Boss, Use the ETHICS Compass

These three Jews were commanded to kiss up to the boss or else. How did these young men stand and not crumple under such incredible pressure? Let's apply the ETHICS Compass to learn how they solved this ethical dilemma.

Examine the Facts

We have learned that the first step in making a proper ethical decision is to carefully examine all of the facts. Undoubtedly, Shadrach, Meshach, and Abednego made sure they had all the facts. There had to have been an incredible buzz in Nebuchadnezzar's office for some time as the gold statue was being built. Also, it must have taken a lot of time to orchestrate the ceremony and gather the musicians. Nebuchadnezzar would certainly have his government employees make all of the arrangements for such a grand affair. Finally, the day arrived when everyone was to come to the dedication ceremony. Rumors and gossip abound in any workplace, and only a fool would have seen what was happening and not figured out the implications. The three Jews knew what was coming.

Rick, in our case study, also needs to sort through the facts. What has he heard? All the salespeople are required to do the following:

- They are to move the old software off the shelves.
- They are to do that by selling the old software to their current clients.
- They are to inform the clients that their current software is obsolete, which is a lie.
- They are then to tell them that they need the "new" (old) software they are offering, which is another lie.
- In the spring, they have to go and sell the real new software by once again telling their clients that the software they just purchased is once again obsolete and they need to purchase new software all over again—more lies!
- If any salesperson does not go along with this plan of deception, he or she will be fired.

Seek the Truth

The second step is to seek what God has to say about this matter. Is it a black-and-white issue or more of a gray issue according to the Bible? Shadrach, Meshach, and Abednego knew these facts:

- Israel was commanded to serve God alone (Exod. 20:3–5).
- Worship of any idol was forbidden (Deut. 5:7–10; 6:14–15).

For Rick, his ethical dilemma was that his company wanted him to deceive his clients. As he examined the Bible, he came across some pivotal verses:

- "Therefore each of you must put off falsehood and speak truthfully to his neighbor, for we are all members of one body" (Eph. 4:25). It is important to note that lying can be either active or passive. Active lying is when we ourselves tell the lie. Passive lying is when we know a lie is being told but we do nothing to refute it. When lying occurs and we are silent, our silence can give it credibility (cf. Ezek. 3:18).

- "The LORD abhors dishonest scales, but accurate weights are his delight" (Prov. 11:1).
- "Better a poor man whose walk is blameless than a fool whose lips are perverse" (Prov. 19:1).
- "Food gained by fraud tastes sweet to a man, but he ends up with a mouth full of gravel" (Prov. 20:17).
- "A fortune made by a lying tongue is a fleeting vapor and a deadly snare" (Prov. 21:6).
- "A good name is more desirable than great riches; to be esteemed is better than silver or gold" (Prov. 22:1).

So Rick's ethical dilemma is a black-and-white decision. When our decision is clearly spelled out by the Bible, what do we do next?

Hesitate

This third step is to see if there is anything about our decision that makes us hesitate before proceeding. Identify why you may be hesitating.

- Is it because you know what the Bible says to do, but you *don't know how* to do it?
- Or is it because you know what the Bible says to do, but you are *afraid* to do it?

These three Jews surely could have had some hesitations about refusing to bow down to the idol. They would be

- publicly disobeying the boss
- publicly embarrassing the boss
- enduring death in a fiery furnace

If they weren't hesitating before, how about when they were dragged in front of a king whose face was as red as the fiery furnace? It's one thing to make a difficult decision with three friends around a flickering lamp at night. The stillness of the night can lead to a steel-hard commitment. But it's quite another thing to have to make the same decision again in the daylight in front of thousands of people, an angry boss, and a furnace so hot that even asbestos wouldn't help!

Notice how the king approached these three troublemakers:

- *"Let's hear your side."* Predictably, the king went into a rage, not only because his employees had disobeyed his order, but because they had also done it in the view of all (Dan. 3:13). And not only was this disrespectful, but it was also disloyal, and he had to deal with it quickly and decisively. Nebuchadnezzar knew they were excellent employees and valued their service. How do we know that? He gave them a second chance, a chance to tell their side and plead for mercy (v. 14). This showed his great respect for these three Jews in spite of his rage.
- *"Last chance."* The king gave them one more chance to obey. The ceremony would start again, and the music would play one more time. This time the three Jews had better bow down and worship the idol. If they didn't, they would die in the fiery furnace. The pressure to conform now had to be intense. Nebuchadnezzar uttered a most significant statement: "But if you do not worship it, you will be thrown immediately into a blazing furnace. Then what god will be able to rescue you from my hand?" (Dan. 3:15).

In our case study, Rick hesitates, for he knows that the Bible teaches that he can't go along with the deception, but he is unsure how to react properly and respectfully. Rick needs to go to the next step for more guidance.

Identify the Greater Good

The fourth step in making a proper ethical decision is to discover the overriding moral obligation—the greater good. Whenever possible, look for a way of fulfilling both obligations. "If it is possible, as far as it depends on you, live at peace with everyone" (Rom. 12:18). However, if two or more moral duties come into unavoidable conflict, we must always follow the greater duty. The three Jews had to discover and obey the higher law that was applicable to their ethical dilemma:

- *Is it loving God more than people?* Loving God was the greatest and highest commandment for Shadrach, Meshach, and Abednego (Deut. 6:5–6).
- *Is it loving people more than things?* This was not applicable to their specific dilemma.
- *Is it loving others more than self?* While they were to love the king more than themselves, they must love God over all others.
- *Is it obeying God over other authorities?* This primary greater good principle guided the three Jews in their decision to refuse to obey the king (Dan. 3:17–18).

Rick also must discover and obey the higher law that is applicable to his ethical dilemma:

- *Is it loving God more than people?* To love God is the greatest and highest commandment (Matt. 22:36–38). While Rick is commanded to love both God and people, his love for God must overrule his love for man. Loving God in this situation means to know the mind of God and obey it fully.
- *Is it loving people more than things?* We should never view the things of this world as treasures and treat people as toys (Matt. 22:39; 1 Tim. 6:17–19). First Timothy 6:17–18 tells us that God has given us things through our jobs to enjoy, but to keep these things in proper perspective. Rick knows that lying to his clients to gain things for himself or his company is wrong.
- *Is it loving others more than self?* While we can love ourselves, we are to love God first, then our neighbor, and finally ourselves (Luke 10:27). The Golden Rule sets a strong pattern to follow in business decisions (Matt. 7:12). So when Rick asks himself, "How would I feel if I were in their shoes?" he knows the ethical choice.
- *Is it obeying God over authority?* Colossians 3:22 tells us to obey our boss ("Slaves, obey your earthly masters in everything; and do it, not only when their eye is on you and to win their favor, but with sincerity of heart and reverence for the Lord"). Since Rick must obey his boss "in everything," must he go along with his company's deception? Don't miss the next verses: Colossians 3:23–24 declares that our true boss is the Lord. "Whatever you do, work at it with all your heart, as working for the Lord, not for men, since you know that you will receive an inheritance from the Lord as a reward. It is the Lord Christ you are serving." Remember in chapter 5, we learned that in a business situation where two bosses disagree with each other, the senior boss must be followed. Since the Lord is the "senior" boss, Rick must obey the Lord rather than his boss on the job.

Rick knows *what* he should do, but *how* should he do it? Is there a way to please both God and his boss? The next step shows the answer to these questions.

Consider Consequences and Creative Alternatives

The fifth step in making a proper ethical decision is to consider two very important questions: First, what will be the consequences of your action? Second, are any creative alternatives available?

The three Jews knew there would be consequences to their decision. Of course, if they refused to bow, they would lose their jobs and their lives via a fiery furnace. However, if they yielded to the pressure and bowed to the idol, they would keep their positions and lives. But it is important to see that they would also lose by yielding. They may keep their positions but would lose their testimony by compromising. But more important, they would lose their clear conscience before God (Acts 24:16).

When facing their ethical dilemma in the workplace, could the three Jews come up with a creative option to wrong directives? To do this they needed to know three things:

1. *The goal.* What was the ultimate goal their boss had for this wrong directive? Primarily, it was to eliminate the Jews' worship of their God and to glorify himself. Nebuchadnezzar clearly stated his goal to the three: "Is it true, Shadrach, Meshach and Abednego, that you do not serve my gods or worship the image of gold I have set up?" (Dan. 3:14).

2. *The better way.* Is there a better way to accomplish the goal? If the goal is good, there can be acceptable alternatives to accomplish it. If the goal is wrong, no creative alternative can be acceptable. These three Jews knew that the goal itself was wrong and that there was no better way to accomplish a wrong goal.

3. *A wise approach.* The presentation of one's ethical position and creative alternative is very important. But if the goal is wrong, then there is no better way to accomplish it and no wise approach to present an alternative.

Like Shadrach, Meshach, and Abednego, Rick needs to consider the consequences of his action and any creative alternatives available.

On the one hand, there will be consequences if Rick does not go along with the boss's plan—she told him he would be out of a job. On the other hand, there will be consequences to following the plan. Rick will have to lie and deceive his clients, he will lose his Christian witness at work that he spent years establishing, and he will violate God's Word.

Can Rick come up with a creative option to wrong directives? To do this, Rick needs to think through Jean's goal, see if there is a better way, and approach her with wisdom.

1. *Goal.* Rick's boss's ultimate goal is to move the old merchandise off the shelves. Most bosses only care about the bottom line of profit. Knowing what the boss ultimately wants is the starting point to solving the problem.

2. *Better way.* Could Rick accomplish the same results using ethical methods? The only way to move old merchandise off the shelves is to sell it at a reduced price. Rick's boss will not hear of such a thing. When Rick privately suggests it to her, she retorts, "That's exactly the kind of closed-minded thinking I would expect from someone like you."

3. *Wise approach.* Rick wisely presents his position and creative alternative when he privately meets with Jean. He uses the Oreo cookie method:

   - *Cookie.* He starts with something he respected in Jean and agrees with her on the ultimate goal: "Jean, I want you to know that I appreciate your desire to turn our company around and make us more profitable. We are known as the company that stands behind what we sell. We have a good reputation even among our competitors, and that makes it a joy to go out and sell for this company. I know you want that to continue."

- *Cream.* Now he shares the negative of his position on this issue. The "cream" of the cookie is a point of confrontation or sharing a differing position. Rick says, "I am deeply bothered by the company's decision to sell old software as new software with inflated prices. I think this is a wrong decision because, when word of it gets out, and it will, we will lose the good reputation we have worked so hard to build. Not only that, we will lose our clients. They will never trust us again. You will also lose me, as I cannot go along with this deception."

- *Cookie.* He finishes by giving Jean the benefit of the doubt and looking for the best in her intent: "You have worked so hard to build your career that it would be a shame to blow it all now. You don't want to end up on the evening news and be seen as a crook. I know that you would rather do the right thing. I believe we still can move the old software, and if you are interested, I'd like to share the sales plan I've worked out." If Jean was wise, she would not resist this approach.

Stand for God

The final step in making a proper ethical decision is to decide to stand for God no matter what. The three Jews decided that they would not bow to an idol no matter what the pressure or threat (Dan. 3:8, 12, 14).

- *Challenge* (Dan. 3:16–18). Once more they were commanded to bow before the idol. With Nebuchadnezzar's demand comes a taunt (v. 15): "What god will be able to rescue you from my hand?" Well, the king would soon find out!

- *Response* (Dan. 3:16). Shadrach, Meshach and Abednego replied to the king, "O Nebuchadnezzar, we do not need to defend ourselves before you in this matter" (v. 16). This response seems abrupt and disrespectful, but their response was to the taunting question of the king. They did not need to defend themselves to the king, because he was not their deliverer. God was their deliverer. He was the one who had delivered his people from bondage in Egypt, who did not allow his people to worship idols, and who had promised to deliver them from the Babylonian captivity (Deut. 30:1–10; Jer. 24:4–7; 27:22; 29:10–14; 32:36–38).

- *Power* (Dan. 3:17). "If we are thrown into the blazing furnace, the God we serve is able to save us from it, and he will rescue us from your hand, O king." The God of these three Jews was able to rescue them from the fiery furnace if he so desired. This was the answer to the king's taunting question.

- *Commitment* (Dan. 3:18). "But even if he does not, we want you to know, O king, that we will not serve your gods or worship the image of gold you have set up." They would not presume that God would deliver them. He could, if he chose to, if it accomplished his will. But even if he did not, the three would not bow down. They believed that, though they may not be saved *from* the fire, they would be saved *in* the fire.

- *Taking the heat* (Dan. 3:19–23). The king's face got even redder. Not only did his three employees refuse to obey, but they did it a second time in front of thousands of his other employees and subjects. So he had the furnace made seven times hotter, and the three brave Jews were thrown in from above, bound hand and foot. They purposed in their hearts that they would stand for God no matter what, and now they got what they wanted.

Rick had to make the same decision as these three Jews. He would stand for God no matter what. He would have to be willing to lose his job, his home, even his security to do the right thing. While this was a hard decision for Rick, it was also very freeing. For once he made this decision, he fulfilled 1 Peter 5:7, which says, "Cast all your anxiety on him because he cares for you." To "cast" here means to throw down at the feet of Christ your cares. Once Rick did this, he knew he was in the hands of God to do as he willed.

Remember That Suffering Leads to Glory

How did the suffering of the three Jews lead to glory?

- *The king's astonishment* (Dan. 3:24–27). Nebuchadnezzar thought this judgment would glorify him, but it ended in glorifying God. As the king looked into the furnace, he was stunned. Not only were the men not consumed by the flames, but there were actually four men, not three, in the furnace. The fourth man the king saw was not human but looked to be divine! He called the men to come out of the furnace, but notice what he called them: "servants of the Most High God" (v. 26). The king acknowledged that the God who could save these men must be the most powerful and important God of all. When the three Jews came out, they were not sizzled or singed. They didn't even smell of smoke.

- *The king's announcement* (Dan. 3:28–30). Nebuchadnezzar praised the God of the Jews and threatened to punish anyone who interfered with their religion. He also promoted Shadrach, Meshach, and Abednego to places of greater importance, with more prosperity.

Rick did suffer. Jean refused Rick's better way as well as his wise rebuking counsel. Angrily, she fired him. For a couple of weeks, things looked pretty bleak, but soon his old clients began contacting him, wondering what had happened to him. All Rick said was that he and the company had parted ways because of a difference of opinion as to how to conduct business. Some told Rick that they had heard a rumor that his former company was pushing old software as new. An investigation had begun to determine who was responsible. While Rick was surprised at the investigation, he said that he did not want to comment. His former clients said that they no longer trusted his old company but wanted him to service them as a consultant.

Within six months, Rick had more clients and was making more money than he ever had before. He also was working for himself. What happened to Rick's former boss? Amid the rumors, an investigation was begun inside and outside the company. Former clients sued, heavy fines were levied, a public scandal broke out, and Rick's boss was terminated.

Conclusion

In the workplace, there will be times when we will face the ethical dilemma of kissing up to the boss or else. If we do yield to the natural temptation to go along, we will violate our ethical standards. If we don't, we may jeopardize our position, our security, and our future. What do we do?

In Daniel 1, Daniel and his friends faced the dilemma of pleasing God *and* man. Fortunately, they were able to please both. In Daniel 3, the issue was whether to please God *or* man. Shadrach, Meshach, and Abednego faced the ethical dilemma of being forced to kiss up to the boss or else. To bow down to the king and his idol would violate their moral standards, as well as their witness. But to refuse to obey the king would mean certain death. These three chose to please God rather than man. While they were punished, they were also delivered by God. Their example of courage and God's demonstration of deliverance should encourage us to bow down to God alone.

Sometimes the pressure to compromise comes from the top, such as from a supervisor on the job. At other times it comes from peers who put tremendous pressure on us to come down to their lower level of ethics. The next chapter will discuss how to overcome peer pressure with power principles.

8

Going with the Flow

"It's easier to get forgiveness than permission." That's a common phrase that encourages many people in business to find ways to overcome the obstacles of bureaucracy, of "red tape," to move a project ahead. If you ask for permission, someone will just say no. So just charge ahead and let the consequences take care of themselves.

Seth will never forget the day when Tom, his boss, who claimed to be a Christian, quoted those words, "It's easier to get forgiveness than permission," to him. What led to this statement was a seemingly insignificant business decision.

Seth works for a company that operates a chain of six restaurants. One week ago, the company's leadership team was having a discussion that centered on one of their restaurants that needs to be remodeled. The exterior of the restaurant is not attractive to customers and needs a new look. A suggestion was made to paint the exterior of the building with brighter colors and to remodel the entrance of the building as well.

The problem is that they do not own the building but rather lease it. Tom, the owner, said, "Unfortunately, the lease agreement I signed stated that nothing could be done to the building without the landlord's permission. I asked the landlord, and she said no. We're stuck."

Everyone groaned and shook their heads.

Dan, the sales manager, said, "Tom, every day we delay we lose customers and money in that restaurant because it looks old and dingy. Plus, the entrance is confusing and unattractive. We've got to do something!"

Bill, the human relations director, spoke up. "Let's just go ahead and remodel and paint the building. Once it's done, what can they do about it?"

"I agree," chimed in Jean of accounting. "If the landlord takes us to court, we'll just paint it back. But that will take time and cost her a lot of money. Trust me; she won't do anything. If she does, we'll simply find a new place."

Everyone agreed except Seth, the operations manager of the company and the one responsible for the overall function of the stores. As a Christian, Seth knew the approach being presented was unethical, not to mention damaging to his Christian testimony. Over time, he had built a good rapport with the landlord and had witnessed to her several times. Seth cleared his throat and said, "I think we need to slow down and rethink this decision. We have been at that location for seven years. We have worked hard to maintain a good relationship with the landlord. Are we to ruin that with one act? We also have a reputation as a Christian company. What would this action do to that?"

Tom had always made a big point to tell others he was a Christian and this was a Christian company. Yet in private, Tom acted like anything but a Christian. When Seth spoke these words, Tom just shook his head.

Everyone else groaned again and lashed out at Seth. "Are you saying we should do nothing?" Dan asked. "That's not an option. You of all people know how sales have declined in that restaurant, especially in the last year. Your idealism is fine for church, but this is business."

Bill said, "Seth, come on. This is nothing personal; it's just business. Sometimes you have to be bold and do things that may not be the best but are necessary. Surely you understand that."

"Seth, your desire to do the right thing is admirable, but if we do not do something drastic with that restaurant fast, we will have to close it," Jean counseled. "Think about the cost. We will lose loyal customers. What about your employees? They will be out of a job. Should you have greater loyalty to the landlord or to your employees, whom you call your friends?"

"But we asked for permission, and we were turned down," Seth countered. "We gave our word in writing that we would abide by her decisions. Doesn't that mean anything?"

"Yes," Tom finally interjected, "it means that it's better to ask for forgiveness than permission." Everyone laughed except Seth.

The decision was made to go ahead with the remodeling as soon as possible. After the meeting, people crowded around Seth, reminding him that he was part of a team and needed to be supportive. He was being pressured to "go with the flow" by his peers. On the way out, Tom put his hand on Seth's arm and said quietly but firmly, "Seth, if you're not on board with this team in this decision, then you're going to be out the door. You have one week to decide. It's your choice."

What should Seth do? The ETHICS compass would help him make the right decision with the right approach.

A New Boss in Town

The ethical dilemma Seth faced was to go along with the crowd at work and take a moral shortcut or else. What did not occur to Seth right away was that someone else had faced a similar dilemma at work. That man was Daniel. As we saw in chapter 6, Daniel wisely handled the ethical dilemma of how to please his boss *and* please God in getting a promotion (Daniel 1). In chapter 7 we saw how three of Daniel's friends, Shadrach, Meshach, and Abednego, handled the ethical dilemma that comes when someone cannot please both God and the boss (Daniel 3). Now in Daniel 6, godly Daniel, a successful leader in national government and an old man, faces the choice either to take a moral shortcut and "go along with the flow" or to end up in the lions' den.

In Daniel 1–4 Nebuchadnezzar was the king. After he died in 562 BC, a succession of kings sat on the throne. Chapter 5 occurs only twenty-five years after chapter 4 (and seventy after the events of chapter 1). Now Belshazzar, Nebuchadnezzar's grandson, sits on the throne. Daniel 5 shares only one day from the life of King Belshazzar—his last day! At the end of chapter 5, Cyrus the Great conquers Babylon and slays Belshazzar.

Darius the Mede, the commander who marched on Babylon for his Persian monarch Cyrus, is rewarded by being placed in charge of Babylon (Dan. 5:31; see also 10:1). Cuneiform texts refer to Darius the Mede as Gubaru, who was appointed governor over all of Babylonia.[1] Daniel refers to Darius as a "king" in 9:1 because Cyrus divided his empire into 120 provinces and appointed a satrap, or governor, to rule each. Each province had been an independent kingdom with its own king. Each new governor, such as Darius, replaced a former king.

When one considers that Darius replaced Belshazzar, king over Nebuchadnezzar's great and enormous kingdom, it is easy to see that Darius was the second greatest ruler in the world at this time, behind Cyrus. We also see that Daniel was correct when he wrote that Darius "received the kingdom" (Dan. 5:31 NASB) and "was made king" (9:1 NASB).[2]

So it was Darius who threw Daniel to the lions, not for doing something *wrong* at work, but for doing something *right*. The scene is set for us in Daniel 6:1–4:

> It pleased Darius to appoint 120 satraps to rule throughout the kingdom, with three administrators over them, one of whom was Daniel. The satraps were made accountable to them so that the king might not suffer loss. Now Daniel so distinguished himself among the administrators and the satraps by his exceptional qualities that the king planned to set him over the whole kingdom. At this, the administrators and the satraps tried to find grounds for charges against Daniel in his conduct of government affairs, but they were unable to do so. They could find no corruption in him, because he was trustworthy and neither corrupt nor negligent.

The Promotion

In Daniel 6, we find that Daniel's old boss, King Belshazzar, is gone and a new boss named Darius is in charge (6:1). This was a hostile takeover and merger to say the least (just read chapter 5)! Daniel's new boss is a pagan who cares nothing for the religion of Daniel or his God. Darius the Mede is the second most powerful man in the world and not one who accepts inferior work, excuses, or insubordination.

Darius appoints 120 governors (satraps) to rule the kingdom. To keep the governors in check, he appoints three commissioners, or federal judges, to rule over the governors. Daniel is one of these three commissioners, but he rises in Darius's esteem so much that he is named top commissioner, with authority over the other two.

The Investigation

Any man or woman in business must wonder, "What did Daniel do to so impress his boss?" Fortunately, we find out, but not in the way one might expect. Before Daniel was promoted, his enemies carefully investigated Daniel's life. This investigation was not to find out if he was qualified, but rather to find some evidence to disqualify him! It was an evil investigation to say the least, as they tried to find some charge they could throw at him. What they found, however, were the three reasons Darius was so impressed with Daniel and wanted to promote him:

1. *He had a spirit of excellence* (6:3). "Now Daniel so distinguished himself among the administrators and the satraps by his exceptional qualities that the king planned to set him over the whole kingdom."

What was it that Darius saw in Daniel? He saw his "exceptional qualities." The Hebrew can be translated "excellent spirit." This means at least two things. First, Daniel had a spirit of excellence in all that he did at work. He was an excellent employee and employer. He was not satisfied with a subpar performance or effort but demanded the best from himself as well as from everyone around him. A person with a spirit of excellence is a rare person indeed in the workplace. This person will stand head and shoulders above everyone else, as Daniel did. This is why Proverbs 22:29 says, "Do you see a man who excels in his work? He will stand before kings; he will not serve before obscure men."

Daniel's spirit of excellence was also seen in his attitude. The New American Standard Bible translates this phrase as "extraordinary spirit." This refers to Daniel's positive attitude and teachable spirit. His positive attitude at work was noticed by others. The king, Daniel's boss, noticed how Daniel responded to his new responsibilities and was planning to reward him by making him the second most powerful man in the kingdom.

It is important to note that Daniel was in a difficult setting. Some readers may respond, "But you don't know how difficult my boss is! You don't know how horrible my co-workers are! I have a terrible job, and I hate going to work!" But think about Daniel's work environment. He was a slave with prestige, but he was still a slave. His country was in bondage. He lived in a godless land, under a pagan man who had absolute power over his life. Also his co-workers were evil schemers who wanted him dead.

But Daniel was a victor, not a victim, and he saw obstacles as opportunities for God's glory to shine through. His attitude was so positive that the king wanted to promote him.

Not only that, but excellence was Daniel's *constant* response. "Distinguished" here is a Hebrew participle that means that Daniel *continually* demonstrated his spirit of excellence.

> 2. *He was ethical in his business dealings* (6:4). "At this, the administrators and the satraps tried to find grounds for charges against Daniel in his conduct of government affairs, but they were unable to do so."

Daniel was honest at work and did an honest day's work. He did not steal from the boss or from others. He was not deceptive in his business practices to profit at another's expense. When Daniel gave his word, people could trust him to keep it, even to his hurt (cf. Ps. 15:4). Ethical excellence, or a "distinguished spirit," was his constant response.

The prophet Micah talks about this kind of character and says that God expects "justice" of us. He expects us to do the right thing. He sums up his message in the statement, "He has showed you, O man, what is good. And what does the LORD require of you? To act justly and to love mercy and to walk humbly with your God" (Micah 6:8).

In this text Micah is talking about the marketplace. Yes, the marketplace! In fact, the very context of Micah 6:6–8 is concerned with economic justice. God asks, "Shall I acquit a man with dishonest scales, with a bag of false weights?" (v. 11). People were cheating their customers when they weighed out the product sold. Daniel would never cheat a person, for he knew that he served God, first and foremost. As Daniel's enemies began their investigation into his business practices, hoping to find some corrupt dealings they could use against him, they came up empty-handed.

> 3. *He had personal integrity* (6:4). "They could find no corruption in him, because he was trustworthy and neither corrupt nor negligent."

Daniel was a man of integrity. His enemies could find no wrongdoing, no sin, and no spiritual lapses in his personal life. Holes are fine for Swiss cheese but not for the Christian! The Old Testament word for "integrity" has the idea of a person who is whole and complete, with no spiritual gaps in his or her life (e.g., see Ps. 7:8; 25:21; and 41:12). Our English word *integrity* comes from the Latin *integritas*, which means "wholeness," "entireness," or "completeness."[3] Daniel was such a man of integrity. He had no holes in his life.

David was another biblical character who displayed such integrity. "David shepherded them with integrity of heart; with skillful hands he led them" (Ps. 78:72). David's heart (his integrity) guided his hands at work. David had no holes in his life, despite his moral lapse with Bathsheba, from which he quickly repented once he was confronted (2 Samuel 11–12; cf. 1 Kings 15:5).

Daniel 6:4 clearly shows Daniel's integrity, both in what was not found in his life as well as in what was. Daniel was found not to have any "corruption" in his life, which means there were no errors or something amiss. "Negligence" was also not found, which means that he was found not to be corrupt, having neither faults nor spiritual decay. There was nothing Daniel's enemies could point to and say, "Aha! Now we've got him!" On the positive side, Daniel was found to be a man who was "trustworthy." In other words, he was faithful in the discharge of his duties. When he said a project would be done, it was done. When he gave his word, he kept it (Ps. 15:4). A trustworthy man is a rare find as Proverbs 20:6 says: "Many a man proclaims his own loyalty, but who can find a trustworthy man?" (NASB). Daniel was certainly impeccable in all of his life.

The Trap

As a worker, Daniel was a man of excellence. He always did his job well. He tried to go above and beyond in his business dealings with others, and the king noticed this. So when Daniel's enemies tailed him, spied on him, and searched through his personal effects, they discovered that nothing was lacking. He had no skeletons in his closet. No hidden dirt. Nothing! Character is not *made* in crisis; it is *revealed* in crisis. Had they found some dirt, they certainly would have tried to use it to blackmail Daniel or to get him fired.

The question that leaps off the pages of Daniel 6 is why Daniel's enemies felt so threatened by his imminent promotion. Why were they so fervent to get rid of him? Of course, they were jealous of him, and they may have had anti-Semitic feelings as well. But the situation seems to show that this was far more serious than that. The reason for their attack had more to do with a business decision than anything else. You see, Daniel's ability threatened them, but more so his honesty. The king was delighted to find a man of ability and honesty, but these very traits were a threat to the corrupt leaders of the kingdom. They could neither corrupt Daniel nor deceive him. So if Daniel was promoted to be their boss, his integrity would mean that their system of corruption, which Darius was trying to correct (Dan. 6:2), would end immediately. A godly man in authority is a threat to the shady dealings of every ungodly man under his authority.

The only "weakness" these enemies could find in Daniel's life was in his consistent worship of his God (Dan. 6:5). So they devised an ingenious trap that would pit Daniel's religious convictions against the government. The enemies got the king to disallow the worship of anyone except him for thirty days. If anyone violated this written law, he would be thrown into a den of hungry lions.

If Daniel chose to follow the pack at work, he would lose his integrity with God. If Daniel chose to follow his God, he would face the consequences. Daniel was in a seemingly unwinnable situation.

The ETHICS Compass and the Lions' Den

Daniel decided to please God rather than his boss. Let's apply the ETHICS Compass to learn how Daniel came to his decision.

Examine the Facts

Daniel did not make his decision without knowing all the facts. He knew that his enemies had devised this crafty plan to trap him (6:5–9). He learned of the requirements of the king's decree that he was not allowed to pray to his God. There was no fog in Daniel's mind about what the facts were or what was required of him.

In our case study, Seth needed to know all the facts before making his decision. He knew the facts not by rumor or gossip, but from the boss's own lips. He knew that his boss expected—no, demanded—that he violate his Christian ethics and lie and deceive to be successful in business. He also knew that his co-workers were pressuring him to "go along with the flow."

Seek the Truth

What did God have to say about this matter? Daniel knew that to pray to anyone or anything other than the Lord God was idolatry (Exod. 34:14; Ps. 81:9). He knew he could not bow his knee to any man or idol. Daniel also knew that he was to pray daily: "Evening, morning and noon I cry out in distress, and he hears my voice" (Ps. 55:17). Daniel knew that he was to pray for God to deliver his people who were held in captivity (1 Kings 8:48–49). Finally, Daniel knew he was to obey God by actually praying for the blessing of the king and kingdom of Babylon. Earlier, Jeremiah had sent a letter to the

Jewish exiles telling them to make the best of their time while in Babylon (Jer. 29:1). In this letter, he told them to pray for the good of Babylon, because if it prospered, they would prosper as well (Jer. 29:4–7). To stop praying for a month was not an option.

Now what did God have to say about Seth's quandary? As Seth sat down and opened his Bible, he found strong counsel about honest dealing:

- He was not to lie or deceive (Exod. 20:16; Lev. 19:11; Col. 3:9).
- A good name is more important than wealth (Prov. 22:1).

Seth was especially drawn to texts about keeping a clear conscience:

- "So I strive always to keep my conscience clear before God and man" (Acts 24:16).
- "I thank God, whom I serve, as my forefathers did, with a clear conscience, as night and day I constantly remember you in my prayers" (2 Tim. 1:3).
- "Pray for us. We are sure that we have a clear conscience and desire to live honorably in every way" (Heb. 13:18).
- "Always be prepared to give an answer to everyone who asks you to give the reason for the hope that you have. But do this with gentleness and respect, keeping a clear conscience, so that those who speak maliciously against your good behavior in Christ may be ashamed of their slander" (1 Peter 3:15–16).

Seth knew that if he went along with the crowd at work, he would not have a clear conscience before God, the landlord, his co-workers, or himself.

Hesitate

Was there anything about Daniel's decision that might have made him hesitate before proceeding with praying? Daniel knew what the Bible had to say about praying, and he also knew how to do it. But he would have had good reason to be afraid to pray—at least for the next thirty days! Darius believed in capital punishment and had a lions' den in place with hungry lions inside. The threat of the lions' den certainly was not an idle one (Dan. 6:7–9). But if Daniel had any hesitations, he did not show them.

Seth undoubtedly had reservations about not going along with the flow at work. Not fitting in at the workplace was one thing, but being perceived as not supporting the company cause was quite another. His decision would be viewed not as a personality issue but rather as a priority issue. So he knew that his job and future were on the line. His hesitancy was not that he did not know what to do, but that he was afraid to do it.

Identify the Greater Good

Daniel needed to identify the greater good and obey the higher law. Thus he had a choice to make: should he obey God or man? The greater good was to obey God over man (Dan. 6:10), which Daniel did.

Seth also needed to identify the greater good and obey the higher law. As he thought this through, three greater goods became obvious:

1. *Love people more than things* (Matt. 22:39; 1 Tim. 6:17–19). Seth knew that lying to people or going back on a contract to gain things is wrong.
2. *Love others more than self* (Matt. 7:12). The Golden Rule made Seth hesitate even more. He asked himself, "How would *I* feel if I were the landlord and saw my tenants remodeling without permission? If I wouldn't want this done to me, then I should not do it to another."
3. *Obey God over obedience to your boss* (Daniel 3; 6; Eph. 6:5–6; Col. 3:22; 1 Peter 2:18). Normally, the good is to obey your boss. But when forced to make a choice; the greater good is to obey God.

Seth knew the overriding moral obligations: God over your boss, people over things, and others before self.

Consider Consequences and Creative Alternatives

This step in making a proper ethical decision is to consider two very important questions: what may be the consequences of your action, and are any creative alternatives available?

Daniel knew the consequences of both disobeying the law and obeying. Of course, he knew that God's law should be obeyed because God commands it. But disobeying God's law does bring negative consequences as well. If he disobeyed the law that prohibited him from praying to his God, he would die. If he obeyed the law, he would lose his testimony before his boss, his evil coworkers, and God.

As he did in chapter 1, could Daniel come up with a creative option to wrong directives? To do so, he needed to know three things:

1. *Goal.* What was the ultimate goal that Darius had for this wrong directive? Darius may have signed the law out of ego, or perhaps he had been duped into thinking that having everyone praying only to him would unify the new country. Either way, the goal of the law was to stop Daniel from praying to his God.
2. *Better way.* Was there a better way to accomplish the goal? As we saw in the last chapter, if a goal is good, there may be many acceptable alternatives to accomplishing it. But if a goal is wrong, no creative alternative

will be acceptable. Daniel knew that the goal itself was wrong and that there was no "better way" to accomplish a wrong goal.

3. *Wise approach.* The goal was wrong, and even the king himself could not change the law once he had signed it (6:8, 12). So Daniel did the only thing he could do—he prayed.

Seth needed to consider these two very important questions as well: What would be the consequences of his action, and were any creative alternatives available?

Like Daniel, Seth knew there would be consequences for both disobeying as well as obeying his boss. If he did not obey his boss, he would be out of a job. But if he went along with his boss's plan, he would be wrong both ethically and morally, not simply because his decision would bring bad consequences, but because it would be an act of disobedience to his God.

Could Seth come up with a creative option to a wrong directive? He ran through the checklist.

1. *Goal.* Seth's boss's ultimate goal was to improve the sales at this particular restaurant. He thought that the problem at this location was purely aesthetics in how the store appeared to the public. Seth had a different perspective. He was in the restaurant enough to hear customers complain about how difficult it was to access the store. Seth had not only studied the financial numbers, but had also carefully studied the demographics of the area surrounding the restaurant. The bottom line was that the problem was not aesthetics but rather location.

2. *Better way.* Tom wanted the restaurant to become profitable. Seth decided the best thing to do was to approach Tom with his concern and a better potential solution.

3. *Wise approach.* Seth decided to present his position and creative alternative in a private meeting with Tom. He used the Oreo cookie method:

   - *Cookie.* Seth began talking with his boss by sharing appreciation and agreement. He said, "Tom, we both agree that this restaurant is not profitable and needs to turn around or else. We both want the same thing. One of the things that I respect about you is that you have a good business eye in that you know what sells, and you also know where to put a restaurant. I have also appreciated the fact that you want our company to be a Christian company and to have a reputation as such in the community. In fact, that is one of the things that drew me here. I know you want that to continue, right?" Tom said, "Of course."
   - *Cream.* Now Seth shared his Oreo cookie cream by saying, "I am deeply bothered by the company's decision to violate our word and remodel this restaurant without approval. Giving your word means something to

me, sir. I think that this is a wrong approach. Not only that, the landlord will take us to court—and win. And we will not have a clear conscience before God if we do this. And finally, I think this is an ineffective answer to the restaurant's problem. The real problem is location, not aesthetics. That is the direction we should be taking."

- *Cookie.* Seth finished by sharing positive intent, "We had a good run at that location, but its time has come. Let's work together and find a better location that will improve sales and keep our Christian testimony intact. Sure, it's cheaper to stay and remodel, but the cost far outweighs the gains. I know that deep down inside of yourself you want to do the right thing."

Stand for God

As in Daniel 1, Daniel made up his mind to stand for God no matter what (6:10–11). Daniel's suffering in the lions' den (vv. 16–20) led to his glory (6:21–28). Daniel's integrity made him a success with his boss and with God (v. 28).

Seth also made up his mind to stand for God no matter what. Unfortunately, Tom rejected Seth's counsel as "poor business thinking." Tom felt that relocating the restaurant was a defeatist attitude and not one he wanted from his company's leadership team. Thus he told Seth that he was to hand in his resignation the next day, to which Seth agreed.

As Seth was leaving the office, Tom spoke up and said, "You know why you and I disagree about ethics in the workplace? It's because you see your job as a place of ministry instead of a place of business. As long as you do that, you will never be a success in business."

Seth smiled and said respectfully, "Tom, I think that you are so wrong in your perspective here. But most important, I think God thinks you're wrong as well."

Seth had to leave the company, and he struggled for a while. But after a few months, he landed a better job that fulfilled his gifts and passion. Tom went ahead and remodeled the restaurant without the landlord's permission, and the landlord took him to court and won. She then kicked him out of her building, so Tom ended up relocating anyway—with a loss of a lot of money and a loss of a clear conscience before God and man.

Conclusion

Daniel's integrity made him a successful businessman. He could be trusted, he had a good attitude in difficult circumstances, he was not corrupt, and he always did his job well. Most people are not like this while at work. In most companies, integrity can allow you to stand head and shoulders above everyone else and be successful.

Some want us to go along with the crowd at work and take a moral short-cut—or else. We always have pressure to "go with the flow" at work, but we must be strong. Both Daniel and Seth faced this same ethical dilemma at work and suffered for taking a stand for God. Yet God rewarded their commitment, and he will reward your commitment to stand for him as well.

What about other ethical dilemmas we face at work? How can we handle the sexual challenges we face at work, such as dealing with sexual temptation, sexual harassment, and other pressures that violate our sexual ethical standards? What about the challenges faced by those who manage people? These challenges range from ethical hiring and firing and fair treatment of employees to maintaining a balanced view of profit. The leader who wrestles well with ethical issues is one whom people can trust and follow.

Employees face significant challenges as well: having a good work ethic, not stealing company time or treasures, getting along with co-workers, and respecting a boss who may not be respectable. Most companies wrestle with the ethical challenges posed by customers. Ethical companies provide a quality product at fair prices and with excellent customer service. Moreover, they tell the truth. Part 4 provides guidance and direction for these ethical dilemmas.

Ethical Dilemmas in Your Workplace

9

Sexual Dilemmas in the Workplace

Howard is a married man with two children who works for a multistate humanitarian organization. His supervisor is an attractive woman in her late thirties who is also married with children. Howard's job often requires trips to the remote locations of the organization, as well as meetings and conferences that are out of town. On occasion, these trips require Howard and his supervisor to travel together.

Howard's employer is a nonprofit organization and is diligent in its efforts to reduce costs. Because of this, the organization will only reimburse mileage for one vehicle. His wife is not happy about the time he spends alone with his supervisor on the road, but his only alternative is to cover separate travel expenses out of his pocket. What should Howard do?

Allen is walking down the hall to his office when he passes Tom's office. A few guys are staring at Tom's computer.

"Allen, come here," Tom calls. "You've got to see this." When he peers over the shoulder of a co-worker, he sees that they are looking at a sexually explicit photo of Tom's girlfriend that he has sent to himself at work. What should Allen do?

Faith is a nurse for a large metropolitan hospital. At the nurses' station, a few nurses are standing at the desk, talking and giggling. Judy calls Faith over to invite her to Judy's bachelorette party. Judy adds that it will be a "naughty" party, complete with male strippers. "If the boys can have fun, so will we."

Judy notices Faith's furrowed brow. "Now Faith, don't be such a prude. Come to my party and have fun." What should Faith do?

Dave finds that he is attracted to a co-worker in his department. She is young, pretty, and fun to be around. She laughs at his jokes, and they have a lot of the same interests. She tells him how gifted and intelligent he is and that he is underused and ignored by their boss. To Dave, her words and presence are like water on parched land. He begins to dress to impress her and wears cologne that she likes. The problem is that Dave is a Christian man who is married with a family. What should Dave do?

The workplace is a mixing bowl of talent, ego, profit, pressure, and lust. Any time men and women mix there is strength and wisdom. There also are interpersonal problems, including romantic inclinations. Fifty years ago, women were rarely in the mix. In 1950 only one in three women (34 percent) was in the workplace. By 1998 nearly three of every five women (60 percent) were employed outside the home.[1]

With the close interaction of men and women has come sexual tension, sexual harassment, and extramarital affairs. There are still some, even today, who do not believe that women should be in the workforce at all. Years ago, a pastor thundered from the pulpit that it was biblically wrong for a woman to work outside the home, to which a chorus of "Amens" rose from the congregation. Yet it seemed an odd statement for him to make since this pastor's secretary was a woman and was not his wife. In fact, most pastors have female secretaries and receptionists. Before we deal with sexual dilemmas in the workplace, we need to respond to that pastor's absolute statement that women should not be in the workplace.

Should Women Be in the Workplace?

It would be wonderful if all mothers could stay at home, especially when they have young children. All should strive to do it. Working or not, mothers and fathers should put their families first, especially the care of children. However, for many reasons it is unrealistic to expect that all women stay out of the workplace. Single women need an income, and some single women have children to support. Many married women must work as well. Increasingly, dual-income families are not working just to buy more toys or to keep up with the Joneses. A lot of couples today need two incomes just to survive.

Besides being unrealistic, a return to a society in which women stayed at home would be unwise. Women are particularly gifted in many areas where their insights and perspectives are needed in today's complex markets. Moreover, it is biblical for women to be in the workplace. Consider, for instance, the Proverbs 31 woman who buys a field (v. 16), has earnings from her work (v. 16), works hard at trading (v. 18), and is a merchant who sells clothes (v. 24). Dorcas (Tabitha), whom Peter raised from the dead, was a seamstress who made fine clothes for a living (Acts 9:36–41). Lydia was a "dealer in purple cloth from the city of Thyatira" and "a worshiper of God" (16:14). Priscilla worked with her husband, Aquila, in tentmaking (18:2–3) and ministry (v. 26). These women were not condemned for working. In fact, they used their contacts for the spread of the gospel.

Finally, don't miss how many times slaves are mentioned (Eph. 6:5–6; Col. 3:22; Titus 2:9; 1 Peter 2:18). Men and women were slaves; whole families were owned. Female slaves did all kinds of chores in their masters' houses and fields. Paul and Peter encouraged all slaves to do the best job they could (see, e.g., Col. 3:23).

The reality is that men and women are both in the workforce to stay, so we need to understand the potential ethical dilemmas that mixing can generate and how to properly respond to them. We need to understand how to deal with the sexual environment of the workplace, with sexual harassment, and with temptation.

Dealing with Sexual Issues

Sometimes walking into the workplace is like strolling the midway of an amusement park. Many sights, smells, and sounds attract and distract. We need to be alert to the hucksters who try to lead us astray. Some of these carnies try to attract us with dirty jokes and stories. They share them in meetings and at the water cooler, always trying to get a laugh. Like amusement park carnies, all they offer are cheap prizes that bring you down to their level.

There are two wrong responses and one correct response when dirty jokes and stories are shared by co-workers. One wrong response is to laugh with the one telling the jokes or stories. That only encourages the jokester to tell more, especially to you. By positively responding to the jokes or stories, you are placing yourself at his or her level.

Paul writes, "But among you there must not be even a hint of sexual immorality, or of any kind of impurity, or of greed, because these are improper for God's holy people. Nor should there be obscenity, foolish talk or coarse joking, which are out of place, but rather thanksgiving" (Eph. 5:3–4). "Course joking" refers to sharing and laughing at dirty jokes that should not be found in the life of Christians.

The other wrong response is to get mad and condemn the storyteller. Such an attack is not a Christlike response (Eph. 4:31; Col. 3:8), and it will only amuse the comedian. Like throwing gasoline on a fire (James 3:5–6), your reaction will encourage more jokes to be told around you by those who just want to laugh at your indignation.

The correct response is to show neither amusement nor anger but to calmly and briefly state the reasons for not telling these stories. Use the Oreo cookie method to confront (see chapter 5). The cream part could be, "Your sexual joke [or story] is inappropriate for the following reasons: As a Christian, it is offensive to me. As a husband and father, you could be talking about my wife or daughters, and that really bothers me. It also creates a hostile environment here at work [see below under 'Dealing with Sexual Harassment']. My counsel to you is to stop, or I will report you."This salty approach (Matt. 5:13) has worked many times and may help you.

At other times, the hucksters offer eye candy to entice. It used to be that the most widespread eye candy in the workplace was adult magazines lying around or nude centerfolds hanging in lockers or on wall calendars. With the influx of women in the workplace as well as the rise of sexual harassment suits, this type of pornography is not as much out in the open as before. Today most office eye candy is pornography on the Internet. In 2004 a survey found that one-third of workers admitted passing along porn at some time. Half of all workers said they had been exposed to sexually explicit material by co-workers, primarily through the Internet.[2]

Some employees spend way too much time on the Internet, and some even send emails containing offensive content to other employees. In companies where Web access isn't filtered, some employees surf pornographic sites at work. Some even send emails to other employees that include videos of people engaged in sex. Most large companies today filter out adult websites from coming into their computer systems. The problem of eye candy still exists but now invades through Web-based emails.

Allen must do three things when offered eye candy:

1. *Remember*. He must remember that what he allows to pass through his eyes will stay in his mind. That is why Jesus cautioned, "Your eye is the lamp of your body. When your eyes are good, your whole body also is full of light. But when they are bad, your body also is full of darkness" (Luke 11:34; see also Matt. 5:28).
2. *Resolve*. Job made the right resolution when he said, "I made a covenant with my eyes not to look lustfully at a girl" (Job 31:1).
3. *Report*. Allen can say something like, "Guys, I wouldn't go to an adult bookstore. Now you're bringing the adult bookstore to our office. This is a violation of company policy, and Tom, if you're caught, I get your chair."

Finally, the carnies at work like to try to get you to visit the "fun house."This refers to a place away from the work site where co-workers gather for a sexually inappropriate event. It could be a bachelor or bachelorette party, such as the one to which Faith was invited in our case study. It could be a bar where the guys go after work to have a few beers and maybe pick up women. It could even be a Christmas office party where liquor flows and inhibitions go.

As a Christian, Faith needs to remember the following verses:

- *She is to protect her reputation.* "But among you there must not be even a hint of sexual immorality, or of any kind of impurity, or of greed, because these are improper for God's holy people" (Eph. 5:3).
- *God's will is that she avoid sexual immorality.* "It is God's will that you should be sanctified: that you should avoid sexual immorality" (1 Thess. 4:3).
- *She is to avoid immorality in all its forms.* "Avoid every kind of evil" (1 Thess. 5:22).
- *She is to actually run from sexual immorality.* "Flee from sexual immorality" (1 Cor. 6:18; 2 Tim. 2:22).
- *She must guard her heart.* "Above all else, guard your heart, for it is the wellspring of life" (Prov. 4:23).

If this is an invitation, such as to an offensive bachelor or bachelorette party or bar hopping, then you have an opportunity to say no, but say it graciously. If attendance is expected, as at an office Christmas party, follow Paul's advice: "Be wise in the way you act toward outsiders; make the most of every opportunity" (Col. 4:5). Attend and see this event as an opportunity to be the salt and light that Jesus commended (Matt. 5:13–16). When Jesus attended social events, he turned them into evangelistic events (Matt. 9:10; Luke 15:2). If the party gets out of hand, graciously make your exit.

Dealing with Sexual Harassment

Sexual harassment in the workplace is primarily encountered by women, though it also happens to men. This is a huge problem:

- Studies estimate that one in four women will experience sexual harassment on the job.[3]
- From 40 to 70 percent of women and from 10 to 20 percent of men have experienced sexual harassment in the workplace.[4]
- Approximately fifteen thousand sexual harassment cases are filed each year with the Equal Employment Opportunity Commission (EEOC). According to the EEOC, the number of sexual harassment complaints filed by men has more than tripled in recent years. About 11 percent of claims are filed by men against female supervisors.

Lindle Beets Jr., PHR (Professional in Human Resources), a nationally certified expert in the field of human resources and leadership development, has helped organizations develop and enforce sexual harassment policies. He says:

Sexual harassment is the subjection of an employee to unwanted sexual contact, propositions, innuendoes, and/or jokes. It is considered a form of sexual discrimination, therefore forbidden under Title VII. The Equal Employment Opportunity Commission cites two forms of sexual harassment that include "Quid Pro Quo" and "Hostile Environment." . . . Under "Quid Pro Quo," a supervisor either threatens an employee with dismissal or adverse job action, or promises some form of advantage if the employee provides some form of sexual services for the supervisor. Under "Hostile Environment," an employer creates conditions or allows actions of a sexual nature that make an employee feel unwelcome or uncomfortable.[5]

Beets says that an employee has recourse if threatened by sexual harassment:

The Anita Hill/Clarence Thomas hearings brought sexual harassment to the forefront of employee relations and law. In a proactive effort to minimize the potential for sexual harassment in the workplace, most employers have adopted comprehensive sexual harassment policies and training. In general, if an employee feels harassed in any way, they should bring it to the employer's attention. If the employer fails to act on the allegation, they will in most cases create a hostile environment. Employees subjected to sexual harassment are protected by federal law under Title VII. If an employer refuses or fails to address a claim of harassment, he/she may want to consider legal counsel.[6]

When facing sexual harassment, understand that you have rights and can appeal to your company for help. If that does not work, you do have the option of legal appeal.

Dealing with Sexual Temptation

A major sexual dilemma faced on the job is temptation. Given that we spend 60 to 70 percent of our waking hours in the workplace, it is only natural that some men and women will develop an attraction to each other.[7] In discussing the pitfalls of an office romance, *The Boston Globe*'s Jason Tuohey reports that anywhere from 40 to 58 percent of workers admit to having had a romantic relationship in the workplace at some point in their careers.[8] Since many people frown on that behavior (and people often lie to survey takers), one wonders if the number is not somewhat higher. Sometimes the relationship can be positive and lead to marriage if both parties are single. But many times the relationship devolves into an uncomfortable situation that triggers disharmony, gossip, complaints of favoritism, retaliation, or even claims of sexual harassment. This is to say nothing of the destroyed marriages, families, and reputations.

In a Society for Human Resource Management (SHRM) white paper, Andrea Poe found that adulterous affairs between co-workers lead to major problems in the workplace.[9] Rob Moll, writing for *Family.org* of Focus on the Family, says that "today's workplace has become the number one spot for married individuals to meet their affair partners."[10]

Moll quotes Shirley Glass in her book *Not "Just Friends"* that "the new infidelity is between people who unwittingly form deep, passionate connections before realizing that they've crossed the line from platonic friendship into romantic love. Eighty-two percent of the 210 unfaithful partners I've treated have had an affair with someone who was, at first, 'just a friend.'"

Glass discovered in her practice from 1991 to 2000 that 50 percent of unfaithful women she treated and about 62 percent of unfaithful men were involved with someone from work. "Today's workplace has become the new danger zone of romantic attraction and opportunity," Glass writes.[11]

The authors of this book, both veteran counselors of those involved in extramarital affairs, agree that most of the affairs brought to us have begun because of work. A related disturbing trend is that even pastoral affairs occur in the workplace, whether the pastor has an affair with his secretary or with a counselee.

Why are so many Christians susceptible to affairs at work? We suggest that the answer is found in the acrostic ODOR—because there is something "smelly" in the home and workplace.

The "OD" applies particularly to men and stands for "Object of Desire." As soon as a man looks at a female co-worker as an object of desire, he opens the door to an affair.

Dave, a man in the workplace, is around women all day who are attractive, energetic, and respectful. But when Dave comes home, his wife is in the kitchen, looking unkempt. There is a spot on her blouse where a child has spit up. She is tired from chasing three small children around all day. She is not respectful as she shoves a toddler in his face and begins to complain about the amount of time he spends at the office. After supper and putting the kids to bed, the only bedtime activity Dave's wife is interested in is sleep. As she goes to bed early, Dave feels like the love has gone. He has no desire for his wife, and his mind begins to think about his "friend" at work who understands him.

"The initial invasion of a lustful thought into our mind is not sin," observes Dave Wyrtzen in *Love without Shame*. "It is when this thought is allowed to give birth to the willful desire to fulfill the act of fornication or adultery that we break God's commandments. We are not defeated simply because the line of a woman's body captures our eyes or generates erotic thoughts."[12]

Dave needs to remember James's warning, "But each one is tempted when, by his own evil desire, he is dragged away and enticed. Then, after desire has conceived, it gives birth to sin; and sin, when it is full-grown, gives birth to death" (James 1:14–15). Jerry Jenkins writes in his book *Hedges*:

> Women leave their husbands for a variety of complex reasons, the most minor of which—according to marriage counselors—is their own lust. Rarely do you hear of a woman who simply fell for someone who, by his sexual appeal alone, turned her heart and head from her own husband. But men—yes, even those who would blame their frumpy, crabby, boring wives for their own roving eyes—don't need an

excuse. They will always point to myriad reasons for having to leave, but it nearly always can be traced to lust, pride, and a false sense of their own strength.[13]

The "OR" of ODOR applies to women and stands for "object of respect." A woman becomes susceptible to an affair when she begins to look upon a man other than her husband with respect. Of course, a woman will not abandon her husband, children, reputation, and future for every man she respects. But a woman is susceptible to an affair when three dynamics are present.

First, she meets a man in the workplace she respects for his wisdom, strength, kindness, and lastly, looks. Psychiatrist Gary Smalley said, "A woman is stimulated more by touch and romantic words. She is far more attracted by a man's personality, while the man is stimulated by sight."[14] We have never known a woman to have an affair with a man she did not respect. Years ago, a pastor was found having an affair with a young, beautiful woman of his congregation. What stunned everyone was that the pastor was old, bald, and fat. But the woman obviously did not see him so.

Second, she feels unfulfilled in her marriage. At home, a man can be unattractive, uncaring, and unromantic. On their days off, some men don't shave and wear holey old shirts. They would rather watch a game on TV than go out for a date. Taken for granted, the wife can be susceptible to a smooth-talking man. If the husband is rude or ignorant of her needs, watch out! Smalley warned a man whose wife had left him that "in cases where a woman has fallen in love with another man or has been severely mistreated, it may take longer to win her back."[15]

Dan's wife, Janet, had left him for another man before he came to Smalley for help. Smalley explained that Dan "could not recognize Janet's need to have a strong and gentle man to support her during times of stress, one who would protect her from some of the 'dirty work.' . . . She needed to be accepted and loved as a person with her own special physical limitations. When Dan repeatedly failed her, she looked elsewhere."[16]

Third, she gives her workplace "friend" some small encouragement to continue pursuing her. She begins to look to him for her acceptance and appreciation. Many men are like wolves hunting for their next meal, and they use those vulnerable feelings to get sexual favors. Whatever his motivation, when a woman responds affirmatively to a man's attentions, it encourages the man and weakens the woman's resolve.

Guardrails against Temptation

How do affairs develop in the workplace? Moll provides some eye-opening observations, among them the dynamic of the "cup of coffee" syndrome: "Men and women begin with safe marriages at home and friendships at work. As they regularly meet for coffee breaks and lunch, these relationships develop into deep friendships. Co-workers come to depend on these coffee rendezvous, and soon they have emotional work friendships and crumbling marriages.[17]

How can we protect ourselves from such temptations? At dangerous highway curves, guardrails are placed to keep drivers from going over the edge of a cliff if they lose control of their vehicle. We need to have guardrails for the heart when at work. Proverbs advises, "Above all else, guard your heart, for it is the wellspring of life" (Prov. 4:23).

Five guardrails in particular can be applied to the workplace. Use the acrostic "GUARD" to remember these principles. These guardrails help to keep you from falling off a cliff when you are tempted to lose control of yourself and have an affair. The principles apply to men and women. Every person who works outside the home needs to know and practice these guardrails to keep from becoming too attracted to a co-worker.

G—Group

Always try to remain in a group, whether in a meeting, dining, or traveling. Don't be alone with an unrelated member of the opposite sex if at all possible. We have tried to impress this rule in discussions with pastoral staff. It isn't always possible to remain in a group in some business activities. Meeting with co-workers, customers, and vendors can require meeting someone of the opposite sex alone. If a two-person conference can't be avoided, make it a public meeting. At the office, leave the door open a crack. Never meet after hours when no one else is around.

Remember that there is safety in numbers. Whether you're a woman or a man, always meet in a safe place—never in a hotel room. You have the right to demand a public setting for any meeting.

What about business meetings at restaurants? If not with a group, these meetings can be problematic. Fine restaurants tend to offer romantic settings, with candlelight and flowing alcohol to lower inhibitions. Even if the parties keep everything totally professional, a restaurant meeting can be misconstrued by others. Just imagine someone telling your spouse that they saw you and a woman in a romantic restaurant drinking wine and laughing. Some business meeting, huh? If meeting at a restaurant, make it a very public event that no one could construe as inappropriate. Always question out loud why a business meeting needs to be held in a dimly lit restaurant. And to protect your judgment and reputation, never drink alcohol.

Here is a suggestion we have found to be quite useful when having a business meeting in a restaurant. When the food comes, pray before eating it. It is interesting how many Christians will pray when surrounded by Christians but seemingly are ashamed to pray around unbelievers. Now don't make a huge public performance of it, like saying, "Let us pray . . ." or even praying out loud.

Just quietly bow your head and pray silently. What do you pray for? Thank the Lord for the food, for the business opportunity, and ask for wisdom as well as protection. By the way, if you are a man, pray before eating your meal whether you are with a group of men or with a woman, and vice versa if you are a woman. But particularly when dining with the opposite sex and you pray for your food, this does two things: first, it says to the other person that you are a follower of Jesus Christ, so he or she doesn't get any ideas! Second, it reminds you that you are a follower of Jesus Christ, so you will act like it.

What is the response? When dining with a group and you begin to pray, usually you will hear someone say, "What's he doing? Oh, he's praying. Everyone be quiet!" When dining with an individual, it is nearly impossible to miss the fact that you are praying. But we have yet to have anyone be disrespectful or discourteous to us for praying. In fact, peoples' responses have been quite the opposite. One of the authors prayed for his food while having a business lunch with an outspoken agnostic. He quietly waited, then said, "I knew that you were a Christian, but I wondered if you would have the resolve to pray in front of me. I respect that you did." This Christian's credibility had increased in the other man's eyes. Not only that, praying before eating your meal may also open the door to a spiritual conversation. On another occasion, after one of the authors had finished silently praying for his food at a business luncheon, the female company president asked if he would "bless her food as well." This he did out loud, and she thanked him. She then began to ask him questions about the Bible, and they spent most of their time talking about spiritual things rather than business. But at the end, she said that she would book the author to speak at her company, and she did.

What about traveling alone with someone of the opposite sex? Remember how Howard struggled with travel that would put him alone with his female boss? What could he do? Always tell your spouse about it and always bring your spouse with you, in a manner of speaking. Jenkins explains:

> My friend used a different hedge when riding alone with a female co-worker. When she asked about him, he pulled out his wallet. Before he showed her the photos of his wife and daughters, he looked at them himself. "It was as though they spoke to me right out of that wallet," he says. "They said, 'Thanks, Daddy, for being faithful to Mom and to us.'" He smiled as he showed her the pictures and spoke lovingly of his family, especially of his wife, Jackie. The conversation mellowed and became friendly in a different sort of way than before. My friend rode with the woman to his hotel, shook her hand, and heard her say in farewell, "Say hi to Jackie for me." "If you think I didn't want to spend the night with her," he admits, "you're crazy." But it sure wasn't worth his spiritual, mental, and family life.[18]

U—Unattainable

You set yourself off in your own attitude as unattainable or "off limits" to anyone but your spouse. No one else can have you because you belong to another.

Paul says, "The wife's body does not belong to her alone but also to her husband. In the same way, the husband's body does not belong to him alone but also to his wife" (1 Cor. 7:4). Sexual relationships with anyone other than your spouse is stealing. Putting yourself off limits closes the door to a predator. Every affair begins when a man or woman regards himself or herself as still available. That opens the door just a little.

Understand that when you said your vows to one another at your wedding, it was not some cute ritual. You were actually entering into a biblical covenant in that you were making vows to your spouse (Prov. 2:17) and to God (Mal. 2:14). Remembering that covenantal partnership with one another and God is important when guarding the heart. Our hearts are deceitful (Jer. 17:9). Out of the heart comes evil thoughts, including sexual immorality (Matt. 15:19). We need to protect ourselves from ourselves.

Wyrtzen writes, "Adultery in the life of one of God's children always causes him to act like the Devil's child. Denial will blind him to the open scandal of his sin, and his attempts to cover the affair will sink him deeper into deception."[19]

A—Ally

Those vulnerable to sexual problems need an ally—someone to stand behind them and support them through the tough times. An ally also cares enough to confront. Whether you are a man or woman, you need an accountability partner in your life to keep you from falling. This should be a strong Christian friend to whom you can talk, reveal, and pray, and one who has your permission to confront you about your heart. Never forget Proverbs 27:17 when it says, "As iron sharpens iron, so one man sharpens another."

Two important points must be made about choosing your ally. First, your ally needs to be a strongly committed and God-centered Christian with whom you can share confidences. This can be your pastor, a good friend, or a co-worker. Because our hearts can deceive us, especially in affairs of the heart, we need the cold, fresh, unblinded eyes of a friend. Second, this ally must be someone of the same sex—no exceptions.

R—Results

You must stop to think about all possible results of your action *before* you engage in it. Considering consequences is part of the ETHICS tool we have been teaching for resolving ethical dilemmas in the workplace. If we would only consider the consequences before we act, we would keep ourselves from a world of trouble. Wyrtzen writes, "Immorality never builds stable homes in which children feel secure. It leads to lies, deception, and violence. The guilt destroys a man and woman physically, emotionally, and spiritually."[20]

We always have time to consider the effects of our actions before falling into immorality. Many men caught in an affair profess, "It just happened!" That is nonsense. An illicit affair does not "just happen." It is cultivated over time with great care and thought. Every time we hear a man proclaim, "It just happened," we can dissect his explanation with a factual examination of his life patterns over the preceding months.

Without exception, we'll find that the man's affair began in his mind months before.

If you are tempted to begin an affair with a co-worker, stop where you are before it is too late. Read Proverbs 7:22–27 and change the seducer into a man or woman, depending on your situation. Don't miss how often Solomon warns that seduction will lead to death. Wyrtzen notes:

> How many husbands in an affair today try to steal pleasure from a forbidden woman when all the enjoyment they could ever want is available in the partner of their youth, who slept next to them for years? Satan calls adultery a destined affair of love. God calls it stealing. It can unleash the fury of violence. Whenever God's principles are despised by ignorance or lethargy it leads to death.[21]

Just try to visualize the following: your spouse has found out about your affair (it never remains private). See the pain, the rejection, and the humiliation in his or her face. Now think about trying to explain the affair to your spouse, to your children, to your parents, and to your church.

Think about trying to explain it to God. If that does not send cold rivers of sweat down your spine, nothing will!

Listen to Solomon again and apply this to the immoral woman or man:

> For these commands are a lamp,
>   this teaching is a light,
> and the corrections of discipline
>   are the way to life,
> keeping you from the immoral woman,
>   from the smooth tongue of the wayward wife.
> Do not lust in your heart after her beauty
>   or let her captivate you with her eyes,
> for the prostitute reduces you to a loaf of bread,
>   and the adulteress preys upon your very life.
> Can a man scoop fire into his lap
>   without his clothes being burned?
> Can a man walk on hot coals
>   without his feet being scorched?
> So is he who sleeps with another man's wife;
>   no one who touches her will go unpunished....
> But a man who commits adultery lacks judgment;
>   whoever does so destroys himself.

Blows and disgrace are his lot,
and his shame will never be wiped away.

Proverbs 6:23–29, 32–33

D—Danger Zones

Know the danger zones. These stretches of highway usually are marked with warning signs such as "Slippery When Wet." The workplace has three danger zones—dangerous thoughts, dangerous words, and dangerous touches.

The first danger zone is strewn with hazardous thoughts. These occur when you begin to have romantic thoughts and feelings about a person other than your spouse. Second Corinthians 10:5 tells us to "take captive every thought to make it obedient to Christ." How do we do this? "Therefore, holy brothers, who share in the heavenly calling, fix your thoughts on Jesus, the apostle and high priest whom we confess" (Heb. 3:1).

The second danger zone is around careless words, as in improper compliments or flirting. One must be very careful about making compliments. Everyone loves a compliment. But many husbands rarely compliment their wives. "When a husband forgets his wife's need for praise, the marriage is usually on its way downhill," observes Smalley.[22]

Being friendly usually involves saying nice things about another person, but one must be careful about how far these compliments go. People can read hidden messages into an innocent comment made to them. They may wonder, "What did he or she mean by that?" or "I think he or she is hitting on me."

A female employee asked the owner of the company if her skirt was too short for the workplace. The owner responded, "With legs like those, you should show them more." He admitted afterward that he did not know why he said that. He knew such a comment was inappropriate, adding, "I'm sure she is now wondering about my intentions."

His friend's response was, "As am I."

The best guideline is to compliment a person's work, accomplishments, or appearance, such as clothes or hairstyle, rather than the person himself or herself.

"Flirting" is a zone of dangerous words. Men and women are susceptible to flattery, which is why predators on the prowl use it. Some people, even Christians, see flirtation as harmless fun. But flirtation sends a message to the other person that you are interested, available for whatever, and thinking about it. Comments such as the following are trouble: "I wish I'd met you before I met my wife/husband." "Hey baby, after work, let's find a quiet place to gaze into each other's eyes." "You're looking hot today."

"The intent of the flirtation is to get another person's attention for romantic reasons, and if you're committed, that's a problem," declares Donna L. Franklin, author of *What's Love Got to Do with It? Understanding and Healing the Rift between Black Men and Women.* Franklin says that flirting becomes cheating from the moment the first signal is sent by someone who is already in a committed relationship.[23]

Flirting is a tool of seduction. A Christian should never seduce anyone other than his or her own spouse. To say, "It's just a bit of fun" or "I didn't mean anything by it" is about as much of an excuse as a drunk driver who kills someone with his car and says, "I never planned for this to happen." He should have planned for this not to happen by not driving to the bar in the first place. A Christian should plan for seduction not to happen by not going there with one's mind or mouth.

What if someone is flirting and making suggestive comments to you? There are four things you must do: First, *recognize the danger.* It's not nice. It's not funny. It's not a compliment. It is danger. Solomon warns of the flirtatious woman. His words can be applied to men or women. He writes, "Say to wisdom, 'You are my sister,' and call understanding your kinsman; they will keep you from the adulteress, from the wayward wife with her seductive words" (Prov. 7:4–5). He describes how the seductress operated: "With persuasive words she led him astray; she seduced him with her smooth talk" (Prov. 7:21). The result of this flirtation was disaster:

> All at once he followed her
>   like an ox going to the slaughter,
> like a deer stepping into a noose
>   till an arrow pierces his liver,
> like a bird darting into a snare,
>   little knowing it will cost him his life.
> Now then, my sons, listen to me;
>   pay attention to what I say.
> Do not let your heart turn to her ways
>   or stray into her paths.
> Many are the victims she has brought down;
>   her slain are a mighty throng.
> Her house is a highway to the grave,
>   leading down to the chambers of death.
>
>   Proverbs 7:22–27

Second, *run to the cross.* Do not allow these words to find a place in your heart. Paul's warning to Timothy is for us as well. "Flee the evil desires of youth, and pursue righteousness, faith, love and peace, along with those who call on the Lord out of a pure heart" (2 Tim. 2:22).

Notice that Paul told Timothy to flee and to pursue. Flee the relationship of lust and pursue the relationship with God. By the way, the "evil desires of youth" describe not age but rather maturity. Why do so many men who are having a "mid-life crisis" have affairs with younger women? They are old in age but immature in controlling their evil, youthful desires.

Third, *confront the person*. Tell the offender in clear terms that these types of comments are unacceptable to you.

Fourth, *report the person if the comments do not stop*. The approach to dealing with dirty jokes or stories works here as well (see pages 107–8).

The third danger zone is found in sensuous touches. This occurs when we touch a person other than our spouse in ways that are too much, too long, or too intimate. Spending time with people at work leads to good friendships. We tend to touch good friends with pats, hugs, maybe a squeeze of a hand. We are not saying that one can never touch a friend of the other gender, but we must be careful about it. The best approach to touching is to only do it in public view. This approach will keep you from touching too long or with too much passion. This sends the message to the other person that this is friendship touching, not romantic touching.

Conclusion

What if you find that you, as a married Christian, are attracted to someone in the workplace? Commit the GUARD rules to memory and practice them daily:

- G—*Group*. Never be alone with the person to whom you are attracted. Never! Infatuation, which is what this is, comes and goes. As long as it is in your heart, be in a group.
- U—*Unavailable*. Remind yourself of your vows. Place pictures of your family everywhere in your workplace. Do not become a thief.
- A—*Ally*. Find someone of the same gender of "iron" and tell the truth. Then make yourself accountable. This may be painful, but it is less painful than a divorce proceeding.
- R—*Results*. Visualize the results/consequences when, not if, your affair becomes public. This should scare you straight.
- D—*Danger zones*. Recognize your danger zones, such as dangerous thoughts, words, or touches. Our advice to you is do not go there! Do not say or do anything you would not do if your husband or wife were there.

We have written this chapter because we have seen the devastation that an affair can have on your marriage, your children, and your testimony for Christ. We plead with you as in Proverbs 4:23 to "guard your heart."

10

Ethical Dilemmas for Employers

"If Jesus were the boss, how would he handle the mess at my office?" Bill asked. He is a member of a group of Christian business owners who meet weekly for prayer, Bible study, and mutual encouragement. "Think about the issues we as business owners face: hiring, firing, compensation, health and safety, making a profit, and being a good leader. Can Jesus give any guidance about these dilemmas?"

Van replied, "Bill, Jesus was a great teacher and ministry leader, but he didn't know anything about running a business."

"I guess you're right," Bill said with a dejected sigh.

Does Jesus know anything about running a business? If Jesus were a boss, how would he hire, fire, and handle other ethical dilemmas with which employers deal? Let's examine what Jesus would know about the workplace. Many picture Jesus more as a monk who spent most of his time isolated in prayer. The reality, however, is that Jesus was very familiar with the marketplace. Consider the following:

He spent his first thirty years in the marketplace (Luke 3:23). He was born in a stable (2:7), which was a part of a place of business much like our modern gas station. His first visitors were blue-collar workers, shepherds (vv. 15–20).

When Jesus began his ministry, he was recognized more as a workman than a teacher. "'Isn't this the carpenter? Isn't this Mary's son and the brother of James, Joseph, Judas and Simon? Aren't his sisters here with us?' And they took offense at him" (Mark 6:3). A carpenter was a builder who worked primarily in wood. Many of his neighbors' homes may have been framed by Jesus. They may have eaten at tables made by Jesus. The yokes for their oxen may have been made by him (see Matt. 11:29–30).

Jesus would have learned his trade as a teen, so by age thirty he had spent ten to fifteen years in the workplace, compared to three years of public ministry. This tells us that Jesus was knowledgeable and comfortable in the workplace.

Jesus called businessmen, not clergy, to be a part of his team. Peter, Andrew, James, and John were fishermen, working in the food industry (Matt. 4:18–22). Nathanael was probably a farmer (John 1:48). Matthew was a tax collector and so a contractor who worked with the government (Matt. 9:9). Even the apostle Paul was a tentmaker, a businessman who constructed temporary housing and supported his ministry through his business (Acts 18:3). Jesus developed this small group of businessmen to be a force that changed the world. Not bad for a simple carpenter!

Not only did Jesus have workplace experience, but much of his ministry was in the workplace. Furthermore, many of his parables were workplace oriented, which shows not only Jesus's knowledge of the ins and outs of the workplace, but also his perspective on it. We will examine some of these parables below.

First, let's see how Jesus dealt with some of the same ethical dilemmas employers face today.

Hiring

How does one hire the right person? One major ethical dilemma faced by private U.S. companies with fifteen or more employees is the Title VII Civil Rights Act of 1964. This legislation outlaws discrimination based on race, color, religion, sex, or national origin. This is applicable to all hiring and firing issues and must be followed carefully.

The primary ethical dilemmas involved in hiring usually come when we hire the wrong person or when we hire in the wrong way. When Jesus called the apostles, he selected an excellent team of leaders and gave us an example we can follow.

Meet a Need with an Opening

To know what sort of employee you are looking for, you must know what your company needs. Jesus knew what the need was and who could fill that need. "Jesus went up on a mountainside and called to him those he wanted, and they came to him" (Mark 3:13). "You did not choose me, but I chose you and appointed you to go and bear fruit," he told his disciples (John 15:16). There is a need that requires a person who can fill the need. Jesus needed apostles to reach the world. When hiring, always start with the need.

Research and Evaluate

You need to evaluate all persons who want to work for you or your company. You must examine their applications and résumés, conduct background checks, and interview them. Jesus did his own research before selecting disciples:

> As Jesus was walking beside the Sea of Galilee, he saw two brothers, Simon called Peter and his brother Andrew. They were casting a net into the lake, for they were fishermen. "Come, follow me," Jesus said, "and I will make you fishers of men." At once they left their nets and followed him. Going on from there, he saw two other brothers, James son of Zebedee and his brother John. They were in a boat with their father Zebedee, preparing their nets. Jesus called them, and immediately they left the boat and their father and followed him.
>
> Matthew 4:18–22

Notice carefully that Jesus "saw" the four brothers and then made the invitation, "Follow me." He saw them as they were working and waited until they were finished with their task. Why? Jesus was observing them to know what kind of men they were and what kind of workers they would be. Jesus did not just choose men without any forethought. He did careful research before making the job offer.

Be Selective

You don't hire every person who wants to join your team. Consider the rich young ruler who wanted to follow Jesus. Jesus told him, "'If you want to be perfect, go, sell your possessions and give to the poor, and you will have treasure in heaven. Then come, follow me.' When the young man heard this, he went away sad, because he had great wealth" (Matt. 19:21–22). Jesus was not saying that a person with wealth could not enter heaven. He was saying to this applicant that his love for Christ had to be more than his love for possessions. Jesus let him go. Three other men who wanted to join Jesus were refused because they had their priorities out of order (Luke 9:57–62).

Pray

When Jesus was ready to select men, he prayed: "One of those days Jesus went out to a mountainside to pray, and spent the night praying to God. When morning came, he called his disciples to him" (Luke 6:12–13). What business book on hiring ever advises you to pray? We know that hiring the right person can make our business a pleasant experience. Hiring the wrong person can make going to work like a visit to the dentist, without novocaine. As Christians, we need God's guidance before making such important decisions. If Jesus felt the need to pray before hiring, how much more should we?

Have a Job Description

Jesus gave his new disciples a very detailed job description. In Matthew 10:1–4, Jesus calls his twelve disciples. The rest of the chapter (vv. 5–42) is the job description.

A good job description tells prospective employees what they are to do if they are hired, why they are to do it, and (in general terms) how they are to do it. It is a written agreement upon which performance will be evaluated. In this job description, Jesus describes where the disciples are to go (Matt. 10:5–6), why they are to go (v. 7), and what they are supposed to do and not do as they go (vv. 8–42). Jesus later did performance evaluations based on their job description when they returned (Luke 10:17–20).

Some companies, especially small ones, do not have job descriptions, and some job descriptions are too formal or general in nature to be helpful. They may describe what the job entails but not how to do the work. Make sure you have a job description for the position you are hiring and that it is as thorough as the one Jesus used.

Train

Jesus constantly trained his disciples (as in Matt. 11:1). A good employer knows that hiring an employee is only the beginning. Jesus spent three years with his disciples, training them by encouragement (see, e.g., John 15:15–16) and by confrontation (see, e.g., Matt. 8:26; 14:31; 16:8). We must do the same.

Relate to Those Hired

Jesus entered into a relationship with the people he hired. Jesus not only selected his disciples, but he also made them his friends. As Christians, we should have a good relationship with our employees.

Firing

We will never forget the first time we had to fire someone in the workplace. When one of the authors had to fire an employee, she leaned forward into his face and angrily said, "And I thought *you* were supposed to be a Christian." Her thought was that a Christian cannot or should not do the difficult things that are sometimes required in the workplace, such as firing someone.

When an employee needs to leave the company, the employer has to do the difficult thing and end the relationship. It may come as a surprise to discover that Jesus had to "fire" disciples from time to time.

Jesus tells a parable about a wise manager who faithfully does his job while his boss is away on a business trip (Luke 12:41–48). When the employer returns, he rewards the manager well (vv. 43–44). Jesus then asks his listeners to imagine that instead of managing faithfully, the manager gets drunk and beats those serving under him. Jesus warns that the one who knows his master's will and does not do what his master wants will be beaten when the master returns. Moreover, "The master of that servant will come on a day when he does not expect him and at an hour he is not aware of. He will cut him to pieces and assign him a place with the unbelievers" (v. 46). The employee is terminated—literally. In Jesus's day, mismanagement of an estate by a slave was a serious offense, and masters could inflict the death penalty.

Of course, Jesus is using an example from the workplace to teach the spiritual truth that unbelievers who do not get ready for the return of the Lord will face eternal judgment. But we should particularly notice two points in this parable. First, Jesus is sharing the reality of the work environment of that day, which included discipline and termination. Second, he does not condemn this reality but rather uses it to illustrate a spiritual principle.

In John 6 we are told about the crowds who were following Jesus. Many people consider themselves disciples or in some way connected to his team. But Jesus knows that the motivation of most of them is not right. So he clearly reveals his expectations and brings his followers to a hard moment when they have to choose whether they are willing to truly believe and follow (vv. 51–58). When they hear his claims, many say, "This is a hard teaching. Who can accept it?" (v. 60). Rather than soft-pedal the truth, Jesus starts eliminating. When they grumble, he asks the challenging question, "Does this offend you?" (v. 61). The result was that "from this time many of his disciples turned back and no longer followed him" (v. 66).

From Jesus's example, we see that firing an employee is not an un-Christian thing to do. Jesus had to send people away from time to time. The primary ethical dilemmas when firing someone center on the *reasons* for terminating and our *approach* in terminating.

The usual reasons for termination are when employees fail to meet the necessary requirements of their positions in the company. The reasons for termination can be:

- *Incompetence.* The employee functions on the job at an unsatisfactory level.
- *Incompatibility.* An employee has difficulties getting along with customers, co-workers, or management.
- *Inactivity.* An employee develops a pattern of being late for work, not showing up for work, taking too much time on breaks, or not doing the job when at work.
- *Unethical.* An employee knowingly violates a company's policy regarding theft or its drug-free workplace policy. If an employee is found to be

stealing, this behavior could result in termination and even arrest. Many companies have a drug-free workplace policy that requires every employee to sign and to comply. Any employee suspected of violating that policy by being under the influence of illegal drugs and/or alcohol will probably be tested. Refusal to take such a test can result in immediate termination for insubordination.

While arbitrary or unethical dismissal is wrong, the decision to fire rests with the company. The actions that lead up to termination can be:

- *Warning.* This warning may be verbal, written, or both. Any warning given that requires an employee be written up for disciplinary reasons should be included in the employee's file.
- *Transfer.* If possible, an employee may be transferred to another position to the benefit of the company and employee. It is the company's decision where an employee is placed.
- *Demotion.* If an employee is not working satisfactorily, he or she may be demoted from his or her current position.

This is a good time to distinguish between an "at-will" employee and a "for-cause" employee. At-will employment can be ended by either the employer or the employee on a moment's notice for any reason. The only exception is if the termination violates federal or state law or company policies. An at-will employee can do little to contest such an action. Nearly two-thirds of American workers have this open-ended employment.[1] For example, every state employee in South Carolina is an at-will employee. At the other extreme, Montana has abolished at-will status for employees of state government.

For-cause employees cannot be discharged without a cause, or legitimate reason, thus the term "for cause." These employees usually work under a contract or bargaining agreement or some other kind of protection. Legally it is much more difficult to fire a for-cause employee. The employer must demonstrate just cause and provide due process to the worker being terminated. The burden of proof is on the employer to show justifiable reasons for termination. In the late 1900s, federal and state legislators tried to address concerns about unjust terminations. The Title VII Civil Rights Act of 1964 was passed to ensure that employers are no longer free to dismiss employees solely on the basis of race, gender, age, or handicap.

An employer who practices Christian ethics in firing an employee is careful about the approach used. Every employee must be treated justly and with dignity. The balance when approaching a termination is to use kindness and truth. You must do the right thing, but you must do it in a merciful way. "Let love and faithfulness never leave you; bind them around your neck, write them on the tablet of your heart. Then you will win favor and a good name in the sight of God and man" (Prov. 3:3–4).

Jesus had this balance, as he was "full of grace and truth" (John 1:14). "Truth" here means to do justice. "Do not pervert justice; do not show partiality to the poor or favoritism to the great, but judge your neighbor fairly" (Lev. 19:15). "It is not good to be partial to the wicked or to deprive the innocent of justice" (Prov. 18:5).

An ethical approach to follow for terminations is reflected in the FIRE acrostic:

- F—*Facts*. Make sure you have a file full of documented evidence and examples for why you are either disciplining or firing this person.
- I—*Identification of issues*. Learn what areas of performance are at issue and the impact of the person's behavior and/or failure on the company.
- R—*Response*. Determine whether termination is the appropriate response to the problems identified.
- E—*Exit strategy*. Direct them as to how to exit the company and property. Explain how they will receive their final check, and other pertinent matters.

A severance package is appropriate for an employee who has served for a significant time or in an important position. Sometimes the job just was not a good fit for the employee, and a severance package will help with the transition to a new job. Consider the principle in the following: "If a fellow Hebrew, a man or a woman, sells himself to you and serves you six years, in the seventh year you must let him go free. And when you release him, do not send him away empty-handed. Supply him liberally from your flock, your threshing floor and your winepress. Give to him as the LORD your God has blessed you" (Deut. 15:12–14). Of course, your decision to provide a severance package depends on the reason the employee is being terminated. If the employee has been caught stealing, obviously a severance package is not warranted.

Compensation

Colossians 4:1 says, "Masters, provide your slaves with what is right and fair, because you know that you also have a Master in heaven." The responsibility for employers is to provide financially in a way that is right and fair. Why? Employers need to remember that they also have a boss who will treat them in the same way.

Jesus says, "The worker deserves his wages" (Luke 10:7). Although this text is specifically about the payment due to those who minister for Christ among us, we can transfer the principle indirectly to other kinds of employment. We should pay those who work for us. No one disagrees with that, but the ethical dilemma comes in how much we should pay an employee. The commonsense principle in business is "You pay the best, you will get (or keep) the best." Yet how many companies have you worked for that followed that philosophy? The philosophy most commonly observed in the workplace seems to be "How cheaply can we pay this person to hire (or keep) him or her?"

Jesus has a lot to say about compensating employees. In three parables, he reveals his compensation strategy. In Luke 12:42–44 he discusses an employer who finds an employee who is loyal, wise, and a leader ("faithful and wise manager"). How does one compensate such a rare find? The employer "will put him in charge of all his possessions" (12:44). This promotion would include a raise in status and compensation. The spiritual interpretation of this parable is to be ready for the Lord when he returns. A workplace application we can draw from this parable is to pay a productive employee well.

In Matthew 20:1–16 Jesus gives a parable of the vineyard. A landowner goes out at 6:00 a.m. and hires workers. He agrees to pay them a denarius, the wage of a Roman soldier, which is good pay for such work. At 9:00 a.m. he hires more workers, but this time he tells them, "I will pay you whatever is right" (v. 4). He needs more workers at noon and still more at 3:00 p.m. and 5:00 p.m. He hires them with the same promise of paying what is right. At 6:00 p.m., the end of the day, he pays all the employees a denarius, even those who have worked only one hour.

The first employees hired are upset because they worked longer than the rest but all have been paid the same (Matt. 20:10–12). The owner's response was that he has not been unfair but has paid them according to their agreement (v. 13). The other workers had come to work for him based on trust, while the first had a negotiated contract. The fact was that their negotiations had actually limited their income because they had restricted the owner's generosity (v. 15). The spiritual interpretation of this parable is about salvation that is equal for all. A workplace application we can draw from this parable is to honor your contracts but be generous. An employer has the right to pay an employee what he deems best or what an employee has agreed to work for.

In Matthew 25:14–29, Jesus shares a third parable about the workplace, which is similar to a parable in Luke 19:11–26. In the Matthew parable, an employer leaves on a long trip and gives his employees responsibilities to take care of while he is gone. He gives each of his three trusted employees the significant monetary sums of five talents, two talents, and one talent. He gives these employees different sums, "each according to his ability" (Matt. 25:15). The master knows his employees well and expects them to perform accordingly.

After he returns from his trip, the employer evaluates the return on his money (Matt. 25:19). The first employee entrusted with five talents has earned five more and is well rewarded. The second employee entrusted with two talents also doubles his sum and is well rewarded (vv. 20–21). But the third employee has hidden his one talent since he fears both his employer and the risk of losing his money (vv. 24–25). The employer's rebuke is threefold: First, he rebukes the employee's character as "wicked" and "lazy" (v. 26). Second, he rebukes his lack of wisdom in business for not investing and producing a profit (v. 27). Third, he has the one talent taken from the employee and given to the one who made the most money (v. 28). The unproductive employee also loses his position (v. 30).

The spiritual principle of this parable is to fulfill responsibilities that the Lord has given us until he returns. A workplace principle we can draw from this parable is to give employees certain responsibilities, do a performance review, and compensate well those who perform well. The employees who do not perform well need to be removed from their responsibility of employment.

Some other verses to consider on compensation are:

- "Do not take advantage of a hired man who is poor and needy, whether he is a brother Israelite or an alien living in one of your towns. Pay him his wages each day before sunset, because he is poor and is counting on it. Otherwise he may cry to the LORD against you, and you will be guilty of sin" (Deut. 24:14–15). We are not to take advantage of those who work for us.
- "'Why have we fasted,' they say, 'and you have not seen it? Why have we humbled ourselves, and you have not noticed?' Yet on the day of your fasting, you do as you please and exploit all your workers" (Isa. 58:3). God takes a dim view of employers who exploit their workers.
- "Woe to him who builds his palace by unrighteousness, his upper rooms by injustice, making his countrymen work for nothing, not paying them for their labor" (Jer. 22:13). A great woe is given to an employer who cheats his workers out of deserved pay.
- "Look! The wages you failed to pay the workmen who mowed your fields are crying out against you. The cries of the harvesters have reached the ears of the Lord Almighty" (James 5:4). James gives a stern warning to employers who mistreat their workers.

Health and Safety

U.S. health and safety issues are difficult and costly ethical issues for employers. Employers are charged by law to provide a safe working environment for their employees. An unsafe working environment can involve such things as unsafe walking and working surfaces and platforms, exposure to toxic and hazardous substances, lack of personal protective equipment, poorly functioning machinery, lack of machine guards, or old or outdated electrical wiring. An unhealthy working environment can also be a "sweatshop," with poorly functioning ventilation or no air conditioning. An unsafe working environment can even include the presence of unsafe employees who threaten the safety of those around them. Unsafe employees can be those with substance abuse problems or with a combative personality. The problem with such a working environment is that those who work in it have no ability to improve their working conditions. They are trapped in this prison, and only the owners have the key.

The Bible gives employers a general principle about providing a safe working environment. "When you build a new house, make a parapet around your roof so that you may not bring the guilt of bloodshed on your house if someone falls from the roof" (Deut. 22:8). While that law was aimed at protecting those who enjoyed cool evening breezes on the flat roofs of homes, the principle is to protect life where people live and work. It means, for example, careful practices on construction sites where scaffolding, ladders, and other factors pose great danger.

If God holds you responsible to provide a safe environment at your home, then this certainly carries over to employers providing a safe environment for employees. The principle here is to provide a safe working environment for those you employ. If you do not and someone is injured, then you are guilty before God.

Does Jesus give any instructions to employers about providing safe working environments for employees? The Golden Rule is applicable: "Do to others as you would have them do to you" (Luke 6:31). Would you work in the conditions in which your employees work? Would you force your children to work under these conditions? If you hesitate to answer, you are violating the Golden Rule.

Jesus also taught that godliness involves treating our neighbors well. In Luke 10, Jesus says, "Love the Lord your God with all your heart and with all your soul and with all your strength and with all your mind" and, "Love your neighbor as yourself" (v. 27). When a man asked who his neighbor was, Jesus answered by telling the well-known parable of the good Samaritan (vv. 30–35). The answer to the question, "Who is my neighbor?" is "Anyone who has a need" (vv. 36–37). Your neighbors are the people around you who are in need. Your employees are your neighbors, and they have a need, which is why they work for you. If you treat them poorly, as by providing an unsafe working environment, you may be breaking government law, and you are certainly breaking God's law. Christian employers and Christian companies should provide the best possible working conditions.

Profit

Is the motivation for profit wrong? What does Jesus know about profit? Most think Jesus was against profit because he said in Luke 16:13, "No servant can serve two masters. Either he will hate the one and love the other, or he will be devoted to the one and despise the other. You cannot serve both God and Money." Luke then describes the reaction of his enemies: "The Pharisees, who loved money, heard all this and were sneering at Jesus" (v. 14). Jesus was not despising money or profit, as we will see. The key to understanding the passage is to discern what masters you, God or money. Is money your tool to serve God and others or your toy to serve only yourself? Riches bring a sense of self-security and self-sufficiency. Jesus was saying that we must serve God and use money, rather than serve money and use God for our benefit.

What about what Jesus said to the rich young ruler? In Matthew 19, a rich young man asked Jesus what he needed to do to have eternal life. Jesus answered:

> "If you want to be perfect, go, sell your possessions and give to the poor, and you will have treasure in heaven. Then come, follow me." When the young man heard this, he went away sad, because he had great wealth. Then Jesus said to his disciples, "I tell you the truth, it is hard for a rich man to enter the kingdom of heaven. Again I tell you, it is easier for a camel to go through the eye of a needle than for a rich man to enter the kingdom of God."
>
> Matthew 19:21–24

Notice that Jesus did not say that it was impossible for a rich person to enter heaven, only hard. As in Luke 16, the question is, what masters you—money or the Lord? There is nothing wrong with possessing money as long as it does not possess us.

Remember that Jesus was a carpenter for much of his life. This was not a hobby he did to unwind or relax. It was his job and provided a living. Jesus had to make a profit as a carpenter. He had to buy goods, provide labor, consider supply and demand, price his work, deal with competitors, and acquire customers. If Joseph had already died, as many believe, then Jesus, the firstborn male, would have had to run the family business and provide for a large family (Matt. 12:46–47).

Jesus understood the importance of profit. We have seen this in some of his parables, where he used the workplace as the setting for his spiritual teaching. In a parable in Matthew 20, a landowner hired workers to work in his vineyard, obviously to make him a profit. In a parable in chapter 21, the owner sent servants to collect his profit from a vineyard (v. 33). In the parable of Matthew 25, the owner expected and rewarded a profit. In Luke 19 a businessman told his employees, "Put this money to work until I come back" (v. 13). There clearly was the expectation of profit. Jesus never condemns money alone, only when it becomes the god a person serves.

The motive for profit to a businessperson is much like the passion for painting to an artist, the singing of a song to a singer, or the competitive spirit to win of an athlete. These passions are what can make them successful. These passions are not wrong but all passions must be channeled correctly. To steal someone's painting or song and pretend it is yours is criminal. To win a race by cheating takes away the integrity of the competition. To profit by unethical means is wrong in God's eyes. The *Living Bible* presents it in this way: "Just tell me what to do and I will do it, Lord. As long as I live I'll wholeheartedly obey. Make me walk along the right paths, for I know how delightful they really are. Help me to prefer obedience to making money!" (Ps. 119:33–36).

Larry Burkett writes, "There is no biblical admonition against making a profit. Profits are the normal by-product of a well-run business and should be considered as normal and admirable. If a business cannot generate profits, it will fail, and its ministry to employees and customers will cease."[2]

Conflict Resolution

One may be surprised at the inclusion of conflict resolution as an ethical dilemma facing employers. It must be addressed for two reasons: First, conflict is common in the workplace. Second, left unresolved, conflict creates an unhealthy work environment. A 2001 *USA Today* article reported that "in your face" rudeness is rampant in the U.S. workplace, so much so that 71 percent of 1,100 workers surveyed said they'd experienced put-downs or outright rude behavior on the job. This conflict, the article said, damaged employees' mental health and lowered a company's productivity.[3]

Did Jesus know anything about conflict in the workplace? Consider how there was constant conflict in the workplace of Jesus. First, there was conflict among the co-workers, the disciples. Either they did not understand (Matt. 16:9, 11; Mark 4:13; Luke 18:34), or they failed (Matt. 8:26; 14:31; 16:8; 17:20), or they fought with one another (Matt. 20:24; Luke 9:46; 22:24). Jesus was patient and loving, but he addressed conflict among them immediately (Matt. 20:25; Luke 9:47–48).

Then there was the conflict caused by angry competitors, the Pharisees and other religious leaders (Mark 15:10). They were competitors because they were trying to get the people to follow them instead of Jesus. To discredit him, they twisted his words or tried to trap him into saying something offensive or incorrect (Matt. 22:15, 18; John 8:6). They also planned to kill him (Matt. 12:14; John 5:18; 7:19, 25). Jesus dealt with these competitors firmly and decisively (e.g., John 8:7–9).

Jesus also had to deal with fickle customers—the crowds. Some followed and believed he was the Messiah (John 4:42; 11:27). Others followed Jesus only to see something new (6:2) or to use him for their own benefit (v. 26). They ended up turning against him. Jesus dealt with his customers wisely (vv. 26–68). Yes, Jesus understood conflict in his workplace.

Part of providing a safe and healthy work environment is to resolve conflict. The employer must set the example by dealing with co-workers, customers, and competitors in a Christlike way. "And masters, treat your slaves in the same way. Do not threaten them, since you know that he who is both their Master and yours is in heaven, and there is no favoritism with him" (Eph. 6:9).

As mentioned in chapter 5, one of the authors teaches conflict resolution skills for businesses in a seminar titled "Office Zoo."[4] This seminar identifies difficult "animals" we face at work, be they co-workers, customers, or clients. I share four "taming tools" to deal with them. These tools help tame our "animals" when they are being difficult and train them not to attack in the future. This training is beneficial to providing a safe and healthy work environment.

Leadership

As a leader, are you a shepherd or goatherd? Leaders face ethical dilemmas in how they lead their people. If you are too hard, employees will hate you. If you are too soft, they will take advantage of you. The balance for the leader is to be a shepherd like Jesus.

In Palestine there are goatherds and shepherds. A goatherd walks behind his flock of goats and beats them with a stick to force them in the direction he wants them to go. A shepherd walks in front of his flock of sheep, and they follow him in the direction he wants them to go. Jesus describes this scene between a shepherd and his sheep. "When he has brought out all his own, he goes on ahead of them, and his sheep follow him because they know his voice. But they will never follow a stranger. They will run away from him because they do not recognize a stranger's voice" (John 10:4–5). Jesus says, "My sheep listen to my voice; I know them, and they follow me" (v. 27).

During the 1960s, Douglas McGregor of MIT's Sloan School of Management coined the terms *Theory X* and *Theory Y* to describe two views of workplace management. Theory X says that people are generally lazy, dislike work, avoid responsibility, and require external stimulus (usually compensation) to perform tasks adequately.[5] Henry Ford said, "The average worker wants a job in which he doesn't have to think."[6]

The job of employers who hold to Theory X is to motivate workers by constant supervision and threats of punishment.

Theory Y is the view that people are usually ambitious and creative, seek responsibility, and can be self-directed.[7] This view assumes that employees will do a good job if given a chance. Employers who hold to Theory Y view their job as one of motivating workers by removing barriers that prevent them from reaching their potential.

Today these theories are seen by some as the extreme ends of the management spectrum, with reality somewhere in the middle. That leads us back to the question of whether one leads as a shepherd or a goatherd. A shepherd leads and knows the direction to take the flock. A shepherd is a leader who loves people and looks for the good things that they are doing. A shepherd does not force the sheep to go anywhere that he or she would not go. A shepherd walks the path first, and the sheep are motivated to follow. Not only will the shepherd die for his sheep, but his sheep will die for their shepherd. Great leaders are shepherds and powerful motivators of their people.

A goatherd also knows the direction in which to move the flock. But a goatherd does not love his or her people but sees them as lazy and dull. The favorite motto of the goatherd is "What is not measured is not managed." While there is some truth in this statement, the goatherd takes it to a micromanaging extreme and looks for the people who are doing something wrong. The goatherd then beats his flock with threats and lack of respect. The only motivation the goats have is to bite at the goatherd or his stick and run away. Welcome to the normal workplace.

A goatherd believes in Theory X all the way. Why are there so many goatherds in business leadership positions? It is because many people seek to exert authority over others because of their training, big ego, or seething anger. Goatherds in leadership usually get away with their threatening, bullying management style because they can. They are in a leadership position and can abuse the people around them.

Christian leaders must become shepherds instead of goatherds. Then and only then will we have the effectiveness of Christ in leading people. Look at what Paul had to say: "You know that the Lord will reward everyone for whatever good he does, whether he is slave or free. And masters, treat your slaves in the same way. Do not threaten them, since you know that he who is both their Master and yours is in heaven, and there is no favoritism with him" (Eph. 6:8–9).

Conclusion

This chapter began with a question: "If Jesus were the boss, how would he handle the mess at my office?" From the example of Christ, we have learned that in our interactions with employees, we need to hire with prayer and wisdom, fire for the right reasons and with the right approach, compensate generously those who have earned it, provide a safe environment, allow for profit, resolve conflict quickly and fairly, and be a leader who is a shepherd. A leader like this will be a person that others will want to follow . . . and will!

11

Ethical Dilemmas for Employees

Consider the following company survey:

Our benefits program is:

1. more than a little generous
2. fair and impartial
3. all the rubber bands you can stuff down your pants

If the office were on fire, I'd immediately grab:

1. important files and key documents
2. valuable machinery/equipment
3. some jumbo marshmallows and a pointy stick

This job has taught me the value of:

1. hard work and sacrifice
2. dedication and enthusiasm
3. lying and blaming others

When I hear the term "company picnic" I think of:

1. a delightful break from the routine
2. a time of fun with fellow workers
3. rifling through people's lunches in the break room fridge

When vacation time rolls around I:

1. make sure all my work is caught up
2. leave detailed instructions for whatever may come along
3. call in sick two days before and three days afterward

All in all, my job makes me want to:

1. sing
2. smile
3. put on a wet suit and shoot fire extinguishers all over

If an important piece of office equipment breaks down, I would:

1. report it to a superior
2. call a repairman
3. declare a holiday

If I discover a large error in the financial records, I:

1. report it to a superior
2. determine the source of the error
3. transfer the excess funds to my personal account

If my boss's expensive European car breaks down, I would:

1. offer him a ride
2. call him a cab
3. tell him he should have bought American

I would rate my boss:

1. the most considerate person I've ever worked for
2. very competent and understanding
3. a nephew of Hitler

If that survey was passed out at your company, what would your answers be? Our attitude toward our boss and job have a dramatic effect on our enjoyment on the job and our success there. Yes, in some jobs the boss acts like a "nephew of Hitler." At some offices, co-workers resemble animals more than humans. But all in all, we need to remember what Charles Swindoll said:

> Words can never adequately convey the incredible impact of our attitude toward life. The longer I live the more convinced I become that life is 10 percent what happens to us and 90 percent how we respond to it.[1]

We have already dealt with several ethical dilemmas employees face: being between a rock and a hard place (chapter 6), kissing up to the boss (chapter 7), going with the flow (chapter 8), and dealing with sexual dilemmas (chapter 9).

For most employees, the most difficult ethical dilemma they face is responding correctly to employers. The Workplace Bully Institute states that the vast majority of workplace bullies (71 percent) are bosses.[2] Why? They have the power, tend to be egocentric, and may be unaccountable to another or others. Five key New Testament passages direct employees in employer relations. We will draw principles from these passages for our jobs.

Although God opposes slavery and Christian principles ultimately overthrew it, nonetheless, the de facto situation of slavery in the first century shows how strongly the Bible stresses servanthood as a role for the Christian employee.

Ephesians 6:5–9

Slaves, obey your earthly masters with respect and fear, and with sincerity of heart, just as you would obey Christ. Obey them not only to win their favor when their eye is on you, but like slaves of Christ, doing the will of God from your heart. Serve wholeheartedly, as if you were serving the Lord, not men, because you know that the Lord will reward everyone for whatever good he does, whether he is slave or free.

And masters, treat your slaves in the same way. Do not threaten them, since you know that he who is both their Master and yours is in heaven, and there is no favoritism with him.

The following observations for the workplace from this text can be made:

- **Position.** *In social position, they were "slaves."* Some translations soften use of the word *slaves* and call them "servants." But Paul uses the Greek word *douloi*, which was used to describe those in subjection and bondage. A *doulos* was truly a slave. If there is any doubt about Paul's meaning, notice that he calls their bosses "masters" and uses the word *kurios*, which is usually translated "lord."

  You may feel like a slave at work, but these people really were slaves.

  What was slavery like in those days? John MacArthur writes that "Roman citizens looked on work as beneath their dignity, and so the entire empire came to function largely by slave power. Slaves were bought, sold, traded, used, and discarded as heartlessly as if they were animals or tools."[3] One Roman writer felt that a slave's only distinction from that of an animal or tool was that a slave could speak.[4]

  In Paul's day, slavery was an established institution with about sixty million slaves in the Roman Empire. "Some historians have estimated that half of the population of the Roman Empire was composed of slaves. Many of these people were educated and cultured, but legally they were not considered persons at all," notes Warren Wiersbe.[5] They were viewed as possessions or tools, with no legal rights whatsoever.

Practically all work was done by slaves. Doctors, teachers, and even the closest friends of the emperors, the secretaries who dealt with letters, appeals, and finance, were slaves. When slaves came to Christ, they may have thought their earthly bondage was eliminated. So when Paul referred to them as "slaves of Christ," he was reminding them that they were still slaves to Christ.

- **Response.** *They were to "obey."* The response of Christian slaves to their earthly masters was to obey. "Obey" translates the Greek word *hupakouō*, which means "to listen under." To obey is to voluntarily place yourself under the authority of your master and listen to what the master says. It is in the present tense, showing that this response of obedience continues for the Christian. Notice that Paul referred to these masters as "earthly," showing that, while their authority was important and to be respected, it was temporary.

- **Extent.** *They were to obey at all times.* They were not to obey just while the boss was watching, to win approval, but at all times. Nor were they to obey only when they felt like it or when their boss was fair and reasonable. They were to obey in everything and at all times.

- **Relationship.** *They were to respond with respect and fear.* The story is told of a rebellious child who was told to sit down. The child responded, "I may be sitting down on the outside, but I'm standing up on the inside!" That wasn't to be the attitude of Christian slaves. They were not to obey just because they had to, but with respect and fear. To show respect is to have a submissive attitude under authority. Paul wrote in Romans 13:5 that we must "submit to the authorities, not only because of possible punishment but also because of conscience." *Fear* in this context means to show honor.

- **Perspective.** *They needed a new perspective.* How could these slaves obey, respect, and honor godless masters? The perspective they were to have was that they were really obeying and serving Christ (Eph. 6:5, 7). This perspective would encourage and enable them to respond appropriately.

- **Serve.** *They were to serve with "sincerity of heart" (Eph. 6:5) and "wholeheartedly" (v. 7).* To serve "wholeheartedly" was to serve with zeal and enthusiasm. This is the attitude of 1 Corinthians 10:31: "So whether you eat or drink or whatever you do, do it all for the glory of God." These slaves were to serve with total passion.

- **Reason.** *They were to look upon their situation as God's plan for them.* Paul told the Ephesians that to work with integrity and a good attitude is the "will of God" (6:6). Our job and our boss are not accidents, but the will of God. Imagine that!

- **Reward.** *They were to await God's reward for pleasing him.* Yes, the Lord will reward us for whatever good we do at work (6:8). A real payday is coming, bigger than any lottery.

COLOSSIANS 3:22–24

Slaves, obey your earthly masters in everything; and do it, not only when their eye is on you and to win their favor, but with sincerity of heart and reverence for the Lord. Whatever you do, work at it with all your heart, as working for the Lord, not for men, since you know that you will receive an inheritance from the Lord as a reward. It is the Lord Christ you are serving.

The following observations about work can be made from Colossians 3:

- **Position.** *They were slaves who had masters.*
- **Response.** *They were to obey.*
- **Extent.** *They were to obey in everything.* They were to serve even when the boss was not watching. They were to obey "in everything" (Col. 3:22). Were they to obey if the boss demanded that they do something illegal or immoral? This question leads us back to the ETHICS acrostic. The *I* point was "Identify the greater good." Sometimes one must ask, "Am I obeying God over authority in this situation?" As mentioned in chapter 5, in a business situation where two bosses disagree with each other, the senior boss must be followed. Since the Lord is the "senior" boss, we must obey the Lord rather than our earthly boss when the two disagree. As Peter said in Acts 5:29, "We must obey God rather than man!"
- **Perspective.** *They were to work as for the Lord.* "It is the Lord Christ you are serving." Paul reminded these slaves that their real boss was Christ.
- **Serve.** *Their heart was to be in their work.* They were to serve with "sincerity of heart" (Col. 3:22). Paul admonished them, whatever the job, "Work at it with all your heart" (v. 23). Sincerity of heart reveals a pure motive. Working at their job with all their heart was to be their passion. The attitude is, "If this is my job, then I will do my best at it and be the best in it." If we truly dislike a boss or job, we are free to leave the company and seek other employment. These slaves were literally stuck at their "pay level." So why did Paul emphasize that they should work with all of their hearts? It pleased the Lord, and it pleased their master. Even a cruel master was impressed with such a worker and would be more prone to treat him or her well than mistreat him. Their value to the master would greatly increase.
- **Reason.** *They are working for the Lord.* Paul said this twice (Col. 3:23–24). As they worked in such a way, they showed reverence for the Lord (v. 22).

- **Reward.** *God will give such workers an inheritance.* Paul reassured these slaves by saying that they would receive a reward from God. All workers need this reassurance.

1 Timothy 6:1–2

All who are under the yoke of slavery should consider their masters worthy of full respect, so that God's name and our teaching may not be slandered. Those who have believing masters are not to show less respect for them because they are brothers. Instead, they are to serve them even better, because those who benefit from their service are believers, and dear to them. These are the things you are to teach and urge on them.

We can draw observations from what Paul tells Timothy:

- **Position.** *They were under the "yoke of slavery," as slaves who had masters.* The word for "masters" is from the Greek word *despotēs,* from which comes the English word *despot.* A despot is an absolute ruler. There was no doubt who was in charge in this workplace.
- **Response.** *They were to consider their masters worthy of full respect.* To "consider" was to count or esteem their masters worthy of respect. This was a choice they had to make.
- **Relationship.** *They had to give "full" or total respect.* Total respect was due even to a boss who was like a despot.
- **Serve.** *They were to serve Christian masters with even more enthusiasm.* Most slaves struggled to serve an unbelieving boss. But here Paul turned the situation around and talked about a slave who had become a Christian serving a boss who also was a believer. Christian slaves might think that they could get away with more or do less because their boss worshiped alongside them. But Paul admonished these believers to serve their believing bosses better.
- **Reason.** *They were to serve to glorify God.* With unbelieving bosses, slaves were to show respect and serve effectively so that "God's name and our teaching may not be slandered." Peter wrote, "Live such good lives among the pagans that, though they accuse you of doing wrong, they may see your good deeds and glorify God on the day he visits us" (1 Peter 2:12). "[Keep] a clear conscience, so that those who speak maliciously against your good behavior in Christ may be ashamed of their slander" (1 Peter 3:16). With believing bosses, these slaves were to serve better because they were dear brothers in Christ with their masters, and their service to help their master prosper also was a benefit to other believers.

Titus 2:9–10

Teach slaves to be subject to their masters in everything, to try to please them, not to talk back to them, and not to steal from them, but to show that they can be fully trusted, so that in every way they will make the teaching about God our Savior attractive.

The following observations for the workplace from this text can be made:

- **Position.** *They were slaves who had masters (despotais).*
- **Response.** *They were to "be subject to" or submit to their masters.* "Submit" comes from *hupotassō*, a military term meaning "to arrange or fall under." To submit, one voluntarily places himself or herself under the authority of another.
- **Extent.** *They were to submit "in everything" (Titus 2:9) and "in every way" (v. 10).*
- **Relationship.** *They were to submit so that they pleased their masters.* A submissive employee responds without talking back. A submissive employee does not steal money and other company possessions. A submissive employee does not steal time by arriving late, leaving early, or taking too much time for breaks. A submissive employee is trustworthy or can be "fully trusted." A boss should be able to trust his Christian employee to keep working, even when no supervisor is around.

1 Peter 2:18–20

Slaves, submit yourselves to your masters with all respect, not only to those who are good and considerate, but also to those who are harsh. For it is commendable if a man bears up under the pain of unjust suffering because he is conscious of God. But how is it to your credit if you receive a beating for doing wrong and endure it? But if you suffer for doing good and you endure it, this is commendable before God.

The following observations can be drawn from 1 Peter 2:

- **Position.** *They are slaves.* He used a different word that can still be translated "slaves": *hoi oiketai.* This term refers to slaves who worked in the house of their master. The term is synonymous with *doulos.* Their boss was a *despotēs.*
- **Response.** *They were to submit by voluntarily placing themselves under the authority of their masters.* The sense of the Greek construction is that Peter was issuing a command to these Christian employees.
- **Extent.** *They were to submit regardless of the character of their masters.* Submitting to good masters is not a difficult thing to do. But we are also to submit to the bad masters. The word translated "harsh" can also mean "crooked." We owe submission even to a boss who is mean or corrupt, or both.
- **Relationship.** *They were to submit "with all respect."* The "all" shows that no half-hearted attitude would do.

- **Reason.** *They were to submit even to harsh masters, because that was commendable to God.* The context of verses 19 and 20 is the workplace. In verse 19 he says it is commendable for a Christian to endure unjust suffering. But in verse 20 he then says that it is no credit to do wrong and then be punished because of it (slaves really were beaten back then). What else would one expect? But if you suffer for doing good and endure it, this will be commendable to God.

If we chart the instructions in these five passages together, we can see the responsibilities of employees. Again, slavery as a political institution is evil but as a spiritual model for voluntary service, Christians have much to learn from it.

	Ephesians 6	Colossians 3	1 Timothy 6	Titus 2	1 Peter 2
Position	Slaves	Slaves	Slaves	Slaves	Slaves
Response	Obey	Obey	Consider	Submit	Submit
Extent	All times	In everything	—	In everything	All masters
Relationship	Respect	—	Respect	Trustworthy	Respect
Perspective	Serve Christ	Serve Christ	—	—	—
Serve	From heart	From heart	Better	—	—
Reason	God's will	For the Lord	Not slander	Attractive	Credit
Reward	For good	Inheritance	—	—	Commendable

Showing Your Boss Some RESPECT

Gathering the principles taught in the five passages, we can see seven core responsibilities that Christian employees must show to their employers. They can best be understood and remembered by the acrostic "RESPECT." Now you may hear Aretha Franklin singing "R-E-S-P-E-C-T, find out what it means to me" in the back of your mind.[6] That's not a bad backdrop for studying the following principles:

Respect

Christian employees are to respect their employers. Respect takes place when we *obey, consider,* and *submit.* To *obey* means to listen to what the boss tells us to do. We are to set an example for others in obeying company policies. To *consider* is a mental choice to respect our boss. Every morning when we drive to work, we need to mentally decide to show respect. Even saying little things like "Yes, sir," or "Yes, ma'am," shows respect. To *submit* is to voluntarily place ourselves under the authority of our boss. We are to respect the good, the bad, and the ugly employer.

If you have a boss who is cruel, abusive, or immoral, you have an option not available to the first-century slaves. You can leave your current job and look for a new one. While we may feel like slaves, we are free people who choose to work for a living. But while you remain in your current job, you must show respect to your boss.

Excellence

In Ephesians 6:7 we are told to serve with our *whole* heart. In Colossians 3:23 we are told to serve with *all* our heart. In 1 Timothy 6:2 we are told to serve *better* than anyone else. This means that, as Christians, we are to be the best employees our boss and company can have. In chapter 8 we saw that Daniel was promoted by Darius because he was an excellent employee (Dan. 6:3). He had a spirit of excellence in all that he did, as well as an excellent attitude. We are to have the same spirit and attitude.

If you would be a worker who strives for excellence on the job, you must cultivate a good work ethic. You show up on time, provide an honest day's work for an honest day's pay, do your job correctly, don't call in sick when you're not sick, and go the extra mile.

A worker of excellence maximizes his or her potential. Become the best you can be at your job. If you are a receptionist, become the best receptionist your company has ever had. Improve at your job. Get on the offense! Improve in your work skills, such as organization, productivity, and conflict resolution. If you want to have an impact for Christ, you must become passionate not just about improving your attitude toward work, but also about improving your work skills. Become an expert in your area. Take classes and seminars, and read books on your field. The more you improve in your work field, the more confidence you will have, the more you will be noticed by your superiors (for the right reasons), and the more you will glorify God. Maximize your potential and be the best employee your boss ever had. You are not to be a slacker or settler but a sizzler! When was the last time you saw someone like that in your workplace?

Service

The service mindset can be seen in 1 Timothy 6:2: "Those who have believing masters are not to show less respect for them because they are brothers. Instead, they are to serve them even better, because those who benefit from their service are believers." When we work at our jobs, this is a service to others because it benefits them. Notice that Paul does not tell us to start serving our master/boss because he or she is a Christian. Rather, he instructs us to "serve them even better." The implication is clear that through our jobs, we serve our bosses, believer or nonbeliever, and they benefit from our service.

One concept we learned in *Bringing Your Faith to Work* was that we are co-workers with God.[7] This is seen in Genesis 2: "Now the LORD God had planted a garden in the east, in Eden; and there he put the man he had formed" (v. 8). "The LORD God took the man and put him in the Garden of Eden to work it and take care of it" (v. 15).

God planted the garden; the man was to cultivate it—the first partnership. We are to manage his creation and care for and meet the needs of his creatures. As we work, we extend God's care to his creatures and environment. We are his hand of blessing on those in need. A nurse is the caring hand of God. A police officer is the just hand of God. A sanitation worker is the cleansing hand of God, preventing disease. A carpenter is the creative hand of God, building things that are both useful and beautiful.[8]

So when you go to work tomorrow, you are serving others and being a benefit to them in different areas of their lives. You are the hand of God being a blessing to his creatures.

Perspective

You really work for Christ. Ephesians 6 says that you are "slaves of Christ" (v. 6) and you serve the Lord (v. 7). Colossians 3 says that you work for the Lord (3:23); "it is the Lord Christ you are serving" (3:24). Paul's point is that while you work for your earthly boss (v. 22), you also work for your heavenly boss. This perspective will provide two things: motivation and reward. Motivation comes from the perspective that we really work for Christ. He sees all that we do—and do not do. It is easy to work hard when the boss is around but to slack off when the boss leaves. Paul tells us not to work like that (Eph. 6:6; Col. 3:22). We are to be working hard all the time because our *real* boss is watching. His eyes are always upon us when we cut corners, surf the Internet on company time, take long breaks, or pad an expense report.

Christ said, "There is nothing concealed that will not be disclosed, or hidden that will not be made known. What you have said in the dark will be heard in the daylight, and what you have whispered in the ear in the inner rooms will be proclaimed from the roofs" (Luke 12:2–3). The perspective that we work for Christ also provides us with the motivation that the God who sees what you do will reward you. That leads to our next point.

Expectation

Ephesians 6 says that "the Lord will reward everyone for whatever good he does, whether he is slave or free" (v. 8). Colossians 3 says that "you know that you will receive an inheritance from the Lord as a reward" (v. 24). How many times have you thought, *No one appreciates what I do around here?* We all have this thought from time to time. Being recognized and appreciated is a huge motivator, a fact that many bosses fail to understand.

The good news is that someone *does* appreciate what we do at work. Christ sees your hard work. He sees your dedication to the job and commitment to excellence. He sees how well you handle difficult customers and the extra hours you invest. We know of store managers who get to their stores at 6:00 a.m., an hour before opening, just to make sure everything is in order and ready for customers. This extra hour is unpaid by the company, but it is not overlooked by God.

Lack of appreciation discourages us from trying hard, so it helps to know that we will be recognized and rewarded one day.

Countercriticism

We are to be respectful employees "so that God's name and our teaching may not be slandered" (1 Tim. 6:1). By being good employees, we "make the teaching about God our Savior attractive" (Titus 2:10). One thing first impressed Daniel's boss about Daniel's God—Daniel's work. One thing that will impress your boss about your God is what kind of worker you are. If you are not a good worker, your boss will be less inclined to hear about Jesus.

One of the authors once witnessed to an unsaved employer, and the employer just shook his head. He said, "Look, I have heard all about Jesus from my Christian employee. She likes to leave me tracts and other literature about God. But as an employee, she is lazy and barely functional. You know, if it were true that Jesus really changes a person, it would be nice if he made them into good employees." It was hard to respond to that, for this employer had a point.

Paul writes to the Corinthian believers, "You yourselves are our letter, written on our hearts, known and read by everybody. You show that you are a letter from Christ, the result of our ministry, written not with ink but with the Spirit of the living God, not on tablets of stone but on tablets of human hearts" (2 Cor. 3:2–3). The old saying is true: We may be the only Bible our co-workers will ever read. By the kind of employee we are, we will preach volumes about Jesus Christ, for good or bad.

Seek the Truth

Look again at the passages of 1 Timothy 6 and Titus 2. First Timothy says to be respectful employees "so that God's name and our *teaching* may not be slandered" (6:1). Titus 2 says that, by being a good employee, we will "make the *teaching* about God our Savior attractive" (v. 10). Paul shares that there was "teaching" about Christ happening in the workplaces, and he did not want it to be discredited by poor actions.

Christian employees have a tremendous opportunity to share their faith about Jesus Christ in the workplace. Our jobs are a key place to be salt and light.[9]

How a Christian works reflects on Jesus Christ, whoever the person's earthly master may be. The purpose of a spotlight that illuminates a statue after dark is to direct attention to the statue, not to the light. People are not inclined to listen to the testimony of a Christian who does shoddy work or constantly complains. If the spotlight is dull or dirty, the statue will not be seen well. If the spotlight is bright and clean, the statue will be seen by all. It will be attractive to a dark world.

The Statue of Liberty is one of the most recognized symbols of the United States. French sculptor Frederic Auguste Bartholdi began the work in 1875 and completed it in July 1884. The statue was dedicated on October 28, 1886, to commemorate the centennial of the United States. The statue's height from its base to the tip of its torch is 151 feet, 1 inch.

Only in the twentieth century, after the invention of airplanes, were people able to see the Statue of Liberty from above. Those who did noticed that the top of Lady Liberty's head is cast in exquisite detail. You can access photographs of the statue on the Internet and examine her head in detail. The craftsmanship in creating the hairstyle for the head of Lady Liberty is incredible. In the nineteenth century, Bartholdi had no idea that anyone would ever see the top of the statue's head. Still, he cast that bronze with the same spirit of excellence that he invested in making her dress, face, and torch, the parts that people would see every day as they approached New York Harbor. What a statement of how we Christians should do our work.

Remember that our Boss sees the top of the statue!

12

Ethical Dilemmas with Customers

"For just $19.99, you can have these miracle weight-loss pills that will literally melt the weight off your body. Buy now! Don't delay!" Infomercials, commercials, and advertisements inundate us daily with tempting get-rich or get-well claims. People who claim to be someone they are not, products with claims that are too good to be true, reports that are biased or misleading—"there is nothing new under the sun" (Eccles. 1:9).

One of the earliest national advertising campaigns began in 1875 and ran for nearly half a century. "Lydia Pinkham's Vegetable Compound" was promoted as the "positive cure for all female complaints" (including everything from menstrual cramps to a prolapsed uterus). Both the bottle and the print advertisement had a photograph of Mrs. Pinkham, the ideal of a gray-haired grandmother. Women provided testimonials of the product's curative powers.

There were three things, however, about which the public was unaware. First, the product was 18 percent alcohol. Second, Lydia Pinkham had died years before the product was marketed. And third, the company spent 75 percent of its revenues on advertising.[1]

Ever hear of a "snake oil salesman"? This concept originated with Joseph Myers of Pugnacity, Nebraska. In the late 1880s, he was helping some Native Americans harvest their medicine plant. They told him that they made a tonic from the plant to treat just about anything: bee stings, rattlesnake and mad-dog bites, infected wounds, and fevers. Myers saw an opportunity and started making his own tonic from the plant, adding in a liberal measure of whiskey. Then he hit the trails, traveling the American West and selling his tonic as a miracle cure-all. He became known as the "snake oil salesman." *Snake oil* has become a catchword for a bogus treatment.[2]

That should have been an ethical dilemma for Joseph Myers, though it probably wasn't. Christians run into false product claims and other issues when dealing with customers. Anyone in business, especially retail, feels the tension between offering a good product and making a profit on it. As we saw in chapter 10, profit is not wrong. In fact, without it, businesses would cease to exist. Jesus understood the importance of profit from his own experience as a businessman. His parables on the workplace recognized the need for profit. The passion for profit is not wrong, but it must be channeled correctly.

The parties involved in making a profit are the seller and the buyer. The seller can be a merchant or a salesperson who wants to sell his or her wares. The seller can also be viewed as someone who gets paid to serve a client or customer, from a customer service representative to a nurse. A nurse gets paid to provide a service to a patient—the customer. If you work for a company and get paid to provide a service that is sold to a customer or client, you are part of the sales process. The buyer is the customer or client, who is looking to purchase something that will improve the quality of his or her life (isn't that why you buy things?). The customer can be a person or company who buys a service from you or your company.

The ethical dilemma comes in dealing with customers honestly, properly, and fairly. At some point, we all have been taken advantage of by an unscrupulous salesperson and then experienced "buyer's remorse," that feeling of regret we get when we know that we have made a poor impulse decision or have been cheated or pressured into an unwise purchase. Christian salespersons should not be involved in causing a customer to experience buyer's remorse.

To SERVE

Christian sales should always deal ethically with customers. The Bible has a lot to say about how sellers are to treat buyers. We have organized these teachings under five core concepts that will guide the businessperson. The acrostic "SERVE" can guide in dealing with customers. The first guideline when dealing with customers is to provide good customer service.

Service

Customer service seems to be a lost cause today. "Bad customer service is everywhere these days—unmanned front desks, surly servers, clueless staff, employees talking on the phone, and managers who refuse to acknowledge a customer. It's no longer an exception . . . poor service has become the norm."[3] *USA Today* reports that in 2005, airlines based in the United States lost ten thousand bags a day, the worst performance since 1990.[4] Who hasn't walked into a fast-food restaurant only to encounter cold food and colder service?

What is customer service? Listen to what Proverbs says: "People curse the man who hoards grain, but blessing crowns him who is willing to sell" (Prov. 11:26). Selling to others out of your abundance or skill is a blessing to others who need or desire what you offer. Serving the customer well provides a crown of blessing. "A good name is to be more desired than great wealth, favor is better than silver and gold" (22:1). Good customer service results in a good reputation. Personal honor and a good name were extremely important to ancient Israelites. Today a disreputable person or company can just pack up and move to another city where no one knows their past. But back when the Proverbs were written, a person's reputation (good or bad) stayed with him or her for life.

What is *good* customer service? These business practices are at least some of the important factors:

- reasonable prices
- friendly service and support staff
- a willingness to go the extra mile
- returning phone calls promptly
- protecting the privacy of personal information such as social security numbers, phone numbers, etc.
- doing what you say you will do, when you say you will do it
- providing high-quality products and services

Art Waller, director of distance learning at Utah State University Salt Lake City campus, has estimated that a typical business hears from only about 4 percent of its dissatisfied customers. The other 96 percent quietly go away. Of this 96 percent, 68 percent never reveal their dissatisfaction because they feel that the owner, manager, or employee does not care. Waller said this statistic is particularly dangerous for businesses. If a dissatisfied customer can't express complaints to a business, he or she will express them to friends, neighbors, and family. A typical dissatisfied customer will tell eight to ten people. One in five will tell twenty people.[5]

"It takes twelve positive service incidents to make up for one negative incident," Waller says. "Seven out of ten complaining customers will do business with you again if you resolve the complaint in their favor. If you resolve it on the spot, 95 percent will do business with you again."[6]

A Christian employee or company should provide good customer service. Most people have gone through at least one bad customer service experience. The Golden Rule should motivate us to ensure that we do not treat others in a negative manner. Recently, one of the authors had to get his brakes fixed. They had moved beyond squeaking and had started grinding. I took my car to a tire and brake shop with a reputation as a Christian company. Initially, I was told that both rotors would have to be replaced, and I was quoted a price. One hour later, the mechanic called and said that he could save the rotors, and the cost of repairs would be half of what had been quoted.

He could have kept that information to himself and pocketed another two hundred dollars. Instead, he gave up some easy money and won a loyal customer. Customer service is not rocket science.

Excellence

In *Business by the Book*, Larry Burkett tells of an interesting incident that has lessons about providing excellent quality. General George Patton had a problem with lazy parachute packers during World War II. Pilots were killed when their chutes did not open because of sloppy packing. An inspection of in-use parachutes showed that as many as 30 percent were improperly packed. In his inimitable style, General Patton charged into the central parachute packing depot and commanded all the packers to take the last chutes they had packed and come with him. He then herded them into a waiting C-46 aircraft and had them jump over the practice range, wearing the chutes they had just packed. He continued this practice for the remainder of the war and never again had a problem with slothful parachute packers.[7]

Sellers deal ethically with customers when they provide a product with excellent quality. Some merchants offer an inferior product to an unsuspecting public. Some employees in manufacturing businesses offer poor service to customers. It only makes common sense to offer a quality product in a quality way. Once it becomes known that your product or service is inferior, no one will buy from you. Or, if there is a General Patton around, you may have to test the quality of your product by jumping out of an airplane.

The Christian businessperson should follow this advice:

> Be sure you know the condition of your flocks,
>   give careful attention to your herds;
> for riches do not endure forever,
>   and a crown is not secure for all generations.
> When the hay is removed and new growth appears
>   and the grass from the hills is gathered in,
> the lambs will provide you with clothing,
>   and the goats with the price of a field.
> You will have plenty of goats' milk
>   to feed you and your family
>   and to nourish your servant girls.

Proverbs 27:23–27

The wise shepherd is to do two things: first, make sure that his flock is in top-quality shape. He is to "know" and "give careful attention" to the quality of his flocks. That way he will get the best price possible for the best quality available. Second, the wise shepherd works on quality now—he does not delay. "Riches will not endure," and his profit "is not secure" forever. Once he works now to provide a quality product, the profit will come as "new grass" and clothing and a field. This diligence is a must for every wise businessperson. Only this will provide riches and a future for his family.

Resolve

Customers who complain can be the bane of a business's existence, so wise managers work hard to resolve issues. As we saw under "Service," if we do not handle a complaint well, the negative publicity they generate will hurt. Proverbs says, "The wise in heart will be called understanding, and sweetness of speech increases persuasiveness" (Prov. 16:21). To resolve a complaint, we need "understanding" and "sweet speech" to persuade the customer to remain after a bad experience. So a customer complaint can be a good thing. Or it can be a bad thing.

A complaint can be a good thing if we find out that something is wrong. A lot of people don't like to complain for fear of "making a scene." The truth is that most businesses prefer that dissatisfied customers complain. This gives them a chance to rectify a situation before it affects others. Plus, the customer will never come back and will bad-mouth the business. A customer complains because he or she wants resolution, but many also want to try to remain a loyal customer. If they walk out the door and never complain, they will never come back. By complaining, they at least try to save the relationship. This puts a positive spin on a negative complaint.

A complaint can also be a good thing in that it gives an opportunity to show that we value our customers. If we respond to the complaint immediately with front-line employees and give value to a disgruntled customer, there is a good chance that we will keep the customer.[8] Think about Proverbs 16:21 again. "Understanding" is acting immediately to resolve a complaint. "Sweetness of speech" is giving some value back to the customer, not just in words but in a discount or credit. This will do wonders to "persuade" a customer to stay.

"If you like us, tell your friends—if you don't—tell us!" This should be the motto of wise businesses that want to make and keep happy customers. You may not have these words written on a sign, but you and your employees had better have them written on your hearts.

A customer complaint can also be a bad thing. You have probably heard the saying "The customer is always right." But those involved in the retail or service industry can tell you that many times the customer is clearly wrong.

A complaint can give a bad customer the opportunity to cheat the business. Bad customers can demoralize employees with their complaints and excessive demands. They can monopolize employees' time and never buy anything. A bad customer is one who files for a rebate and then returns the garment. A bad customer buys a garment, wears it with the tags attached, and then returns it for a refund. A bad customer can even be a demanding patient or someone in the patient's family who thinks that he or she is the only patient the nurse has to care for.

Many companies "fire" their bad customers because of the costs they bring. Retailers such as Staples, Limited Brands, and Best Buy are using technology to identify and refuse shoppers who abuse store policies.[9] Larry Seldon, a consultant for Best Buy, labels bad customers as "demon customers." He even wrote a book on the subject, *Angel Customers and Demon Customers.* Seldon counseled Best Buy to identify and fire bad customers.[10]

How can a Christian respond to bad customers? For two years, I (Randy) ran the third largest chain of dry cleaning stores in South Carolina. One of my responsibilities was handling customer complaints that could not be resolved in the store. I came up with the "three Cs" of customer complaints: Some customers are *correct.* Yes, we had accidentally damaged their shirt. We would reimburse them with a check for a new shirt or store credit, depending on the age of the garment.

Some customers are *confused.* In my experience, these thought that we had lost a garment when it had not entered our stores. We joked that there must be a sign in people's bedrooms that says, "If it's not in the closet, it must be at the cleaner's." Our process and procedures were intricately developed and followed so that we could show exactly what garments came into our stores and when, down to the make and color.

Some customers are *conniving.* They are out to cheat the business.

There are two ethical responses to take when dealing with customer complaints. First, determine the facts. This requires an investigation that may take time. If you have a restaurant and a customer complains that his steak was not done correctly, that is easy to resolve. If you are a nurse and a patient complains that she did not receive her medications for the day, that needs to be investigated before you give her more. If you are a retail operation and have a complaint policy (and you should), then follow it. If the customer demands an immediate resolution, this could be a warning flag that something is not right with their complaint. "A truthful witness does not deceive, but a false witness pours out lies" (Prov. 14:5). An honest person will not object to some time being needed to investigate the problem. As employees, we are stewards of the company and are to protect it as best we can for the owner. If someone is cheating us, we are under no ethical obligation to reward their actions.

But what do you do when you know you are not wrong, but the customer believes that you are? The second response is when in doubt, be generous. Consider the following verses: "The generous man will be prosperous, and he who waters will himself be watered" (Prov. 11:25). God will reward your generosity, even though you did nothing wrong. "Do not repay anyone evil for evil. Be careful to do what is right in the eyes of everybody. If it is possible, as far as it depends on you, live at peace with everyone" (Rom. 12:17–18). Dealing with customers who complain is one of the most difficult things about working with the public. Romans 12 tells us to do the right thing and yield for the side of peace.

Veracity

Honest sellers have veracity. They tell the truth about their products. We all want to make a sale or see an increase in our profits. We may laugh at the "snake oil" salesmen on infomercials and at the people who buy from them. But anyone who sells is tempted to become a "snake oil" salesperson. We are tempted to stretch the truth or to make customers think they need what we offer.

Many businesses feel that exaggeration is morally permissible where no harm results. For example, a shampoo ad says that this product makes hair "ten times softer" than the competitors'. A skin cream is said to make skin look and feel twelve years younger. Ralston Purina was sued by ALPO Petfoods because Ralston Purina was advertising that its Puppy Chow helped to reduce "canine hip dysplasia" when there was no evidence to support such claims.[11] Judge Janet C. Hall, United States District Court, District of Connecticut, issued an injunction on May 31, 2005, against Gillette, demanding that they immediately stop making claims that were "greatly exaggerated" and "literally false" on its M3 Power Razor package.[12]

Scripture cautions against exaggerating claims about a product. "If you sell land to one of your countrymen or buy any from him, do not take advantage of each other" (Lev. 25:14). In selling or buying, we are not to take advantage of others. The Hebrew word here for "take advantage of" means to oppress or to do violence against. When we have been cheated, we say we have been "ripped off."

"Better a little with righteousness than much gain with injustice" (Prov. 16:8). If we gain a lot of wealth because we are dishonest in selling, we will have a guilty conscience and fear the exposure of our dishonesty. An ethical Christian understands this proverb and lives by it. "Food gained by fraud tastes sweet to a man, but he ends up with a mouth full of gravel" (20:17).

"'It's no good, it's no good!' says the buyer; then off he goes and boasts about his purchase" (Prov. 20:14). This sadly humorous exchange reminds us of stores that advertise "specials" just to get customers in the store, then tell the customers that the special stock has been sold. A higher-priced product must instead be purchased.

A rabbinic proverb says, "When a fool goes to market, the merchants rejoice."[13] But dishonesty is bad business. Consider the following verses from Proverbs: "Ill-gotten treasures are of no value" (10:2); "Dishonest money dwindles away"

(13:11); "A greedy man brings trouble to his family" (15:27); "Better to be poor than a liar" (19:22); "A fortune made by a lying tongue is a fleeting vapor and a deadly snare" (21:6); "He who hates ill-gotten gain will enjoy a long life" (28:16). Offer a good product and tell the truth about it.

Ethical

The final guideline in our SERVE acrostic for dealing with customers is to be *ethical* in all dealings. Customers can be overcharged without even knowing it. Butchers can put their thumb on the scale. Potato chip bags are packed to look large but when opened are less than half full.

Have you ever heard about "scanner scamming"? It's when the price on the scanner doesn't match the price on the store shelf and the customer gets overcharged. This is particularly a serious problem with grocery stores because customers purchase a large number of low-priced items and are often in a hurry. In February 2006, Illinois lieutenant governor Pat Quinn proposed a tough retail consumer law with harsh penalties for stores caught in scanner error. Quinn says, "The ones [scanner errors] you don't catch are the 50 cents. The dollar and a half. The $3. Today, mothers and fathers are both working—[they] dash into stores, boom, pay, out again." Quinn said that a Federal Trade Commission report shows that scanner errors cost consumers billions of dollars every year.[14]

Being scammed is nothing new. God condemns overcharging the poor and undercharging the rich. The way the deceptive merchant did this was to use a false set of standards or weights. Often the rich would have their own sets of weights. They were what we would call today "informed customers." They read *Consumer Reports* and knew what the item should cost. Thus, the merchant could not cheat them and they were forced to use the proper weights. But with the poor or uninformed, the merchants would use a different set of weights that would overcharge the unsuspecting. And the merchant would laugh all the way to the bank. Notice how often God talks about this:

> Do not use dishonest standards when measuring length, weight or quantity. Use honest scales and honest weights, an honest ephah and an honest hin. I am the Lord your God, who brought you out of Egypt.
>
> Leviticus 19:35–36

> Do not have two differing weights in your bag—one heavy, one light. Do not have two differing measures in your house—one large, one small. You must have accurate and honest weights and measures, so that you may live long in the land the Lord your God is giving you. For the Lord your God detests anyone who does these things, anyone who deals dishonestly.
>
> Deuteronomy 25:13–16

The LORD abhors dishonest scales, but accurate weights are his delight.

Proverbs 11:1; 16:11; 20:10; 20:23

The merchant uses dishonest scales; he loves to defraud.

Hosea 12:7

God not only condemns overcharging by using deceptive pricing techniques. He also condemns the result of such practices, which overly burden the needy, who were the ones who least could afford it. Dishonest manipulators were the direct cause of some of the poor becoming slaves. Let's see how this could happen:

Hear this, you who trample the needy and do away with the poor of the land, saying, "When will the New Moon be over that we may sell grain, and the Sabbath be ended that we may market wheat?"—skimping the measure, boosting the price and cheating with dishonest scales, buying the poor with silver and the needy for a pair of sandals, selling even the sweepings with the wheat. The LORD has sworn by the Pride of Jacob: "I will never forget anything they have done."

Amos 8:4–7

Let's examine this significant passage carefully. Notice that the rich merchants are charged with "trampling the needy" and "eliminating the poor." How did they do such a thing? In verse 5, we see their heart when they ask, "When will the New Moon and the Sabbath be over?" The beginning of each month was a feast day, a day of rest from work, and was equal to a Sabbath. The merchants had to appear religious and worship on such days. But inwardly they could not wait until they could get back to the business of exploiting people, because time is money!

They were fixing the prices in a devious way. They diminished or skimped the measure on an ephah, a dry measure similar to a bushel. They increased the shekel, boosting the price. The shekel was a weight by which money was weighed. Thus they fixed their scales to cheat. Merchants gave customers less and charged more for their wares. They cheated people, especially the poor, who knew no better or could do nothing about it.

In verse 6, the picture of these predators gets even worse. They knowingly trap the poor so they can get rich by using them. The merchants would give the poor food on credit, knowing full well that the people could not pay them back. Then they would call due the debt. The poor debtor would become the property of the merchant, who would in turn sell the debtor into slavery for a few silver coins or even a pair of sandals. They would even sell dirty wheat for a profit. These kinds of people would do anything to anybody for a buck. Ever deal with people like that?

Businesses that prey on the poor exist even today. Some rental centers suck poor people in with the chance to have nice furniture or appliances. But the monthly charges set by the contract far exceed the cost of buying new furniture or appliances outright. Credit card companies that have very high interest rates lure people into spending more and putting off paying until later. All the while these companies get richer and the poor get poorer.

To the world, the richer you are, the more popular you are. It knows or cares little about how you got rich, only that you *are* rich. In verse 7, God makes it clear what he thinks of such behavior. He will not forget "anything" they have done. When God conducts the audit of these businesspeople, it won't be pretty. How will your own "audit" by God turn out?

What did Jesus think of those who took advantage of the poor just to make a profit? Look at Matthew 21: "Jesus entered the temple area and drove out all who were buying and selling there. He overturned the tables of the money changers and the benches of those selling doves. 'It is written,' he said to them, "'My house will be called a house of prayer,' but you are making it a 'den of robbers'" (vv. 12–13).

Jesus walked into the temple, the supreme place of Jewish worship. Jesus then overturned the tables and booths of the money changers and merchants. Why? To worship, the Jews needed animals to sacrifice at the altars. To make it more convenient, merchants offered these animals for sale right in the temple court. However, what got Jesus angry was that they overcharged worshipers, and the religious leaders did nothing to stop it. Why? Because the religious leaders were getting a cut of the take for allowing the merchants to do business in the temple. Thieves were robbing thieves who were robbing the poor!

Rather than being a place of worship, the temple had become a place of extortionists who robbed the poor worshipers in the sight of all. Jesus hated practices that had turned the temple into a place of business and a place for cheating the poor.

Conclusion

When we enter the marketplace and deal with customers, it can be a "win-win" experience. It is a "win" because we get to sell something that we make or can do. It can also be a "win" as the customer gets something needed or desired. But when dealing with customers, all sorts of ethical dilemmas come our way. How can we handle these properly as Christians? That is where the SERVE acrostic comes in.

What have we learned from the SERVE principles? As Christians, we should provide good customer service, as that is how we ourselves would want to be served. The quality of our products and service should be excellent. As best we can, we should try to resolve customer complaints quickly and honestly. When we tell others about our product, we must tell the truth. If the truth does not sell our products, we should not be selling them. Finally, when we offer a product or a service, we should offer a fair price for a good product. God expects us to be fair. If our scanners overcharge the customer, we should not need a law to force us to fix the scanners. That is what being a Christian in the workplace is all about.

13

Ethical Dilemmas with Balancing Work and the Home

Bob Cratchit took a deep breath and approached his boss. "Um, Mr. Scrooge, sir?"

"What is it, Cratchit?" Ebenezer Scrooge snapped. "Sir," Bob stammered, "tomorrow is Christmas, and I was wondering if I could have the day off to spend with my family. We work so late that by the time I get home, the kids are already in bed. My son, Tiny Tim, is very sick, and we're not sure how many more Christmases we'll have with him. Most of our clients will stay home with their families, so there won't be much business to conduct. Please, sir, it's just one day of the year."

Scrooge sat up from his counting table, took off his glasses, and glared at Cratchit. "Let me get this straight. You want to stay home from work tomorrow to spend Christmas with your family? Who is going to answer the phone, Cratchit? Who is going to deal with all those whiny customers? If we are closed, people will have a one-day extension on their loan payments. That's bad business, Cratchit. No, you come to work tomorrow and be merry that you have a job."

Bob knew that once Mr. Scrooge made a decision, it was final. It was hard working for a man like Ebenezer Scrooge. Bob worked twelve-hour days for very low pay. Not only that, but Mr. Scrooge was a workaholic without a family, so he had no place to go but to work. Now Bob had to go home and tell Mrs. Cratchit the bad news.

Understandably, Mrs. Cratchit was quite upset. "I wish I had him here right now," she sputtered; "I'd give him a piece of my mind! You've got to make some changes, Bob. You spend so much time at work, you don't even know your kids anymore."

"But I'm working so hard to provide a house for you and the kids," Bob countered.

"What good is providing a house when what you need to be providing is a home?" Mrs. Cratchit shot back. "I don't want to talk about it anymore. You go tell your children that you will miss Christmas with them again!" With that, she ran crying into the bedroom.

That night Bob was exhausted, but he couldn't sleep. He wrestled with questions and thoughts like "Why am I doing all of this?" "Is it really worth it?" "I wish I could take evenings off to be with my family." Bob then shuddered as he could almost hear Mr. Scrooge scream, "Cratchit, get back here or else!" As he turned and looked at the sleeping form of his wife, Bob wondered, "But what will happen with my family if I don't cut back?"

Bob Cratchit's struggle of balancing time at work and home is not uncommon. Most workers wrestle with the time balance between work and home. It's worse when both parents work. In North America, nearly half of all families have two wage earners. Less than one-fifth of families are "traditional," with the husband as breadwinner and the wife as homemaker. Seventy percent of mothers with children work at least part-time.[1] A May 14, 2006, CBS News poll found that 68 percent of women see a conflict between working and raising a family.[2] This means that major challenges exist for workers who also have a family.

David Lewis, a stress consultant who did research for an October 2005 study for Pendaflex, said his study reveals that 48 percent of American workers report high stress, and 52 percent say they have an overly heavy workload. Half of the workers said they work late two or three times a week. Lewis stated that seventy-two million Americans face health risks for ulcers, strokes, and heart attacks at work. He cites a "cocktail of long hours and result-driven work cultures" in a phenomenon he calls the "psychologically toxic" office. That atmosphere can include unreasonable bosses, unrealistic deadlines, bad organization, colleagues not working as a team, and a highly competitive climate of people chasing top jobs.[3]

Paul Lewis, author of *The 5ive Key Habits of Smart Dads*, surveyed men on what their greatest fathering frustrations were. Their most common answers are variations on their lack of time:

- not having enough time with their children,
- trying to get away from their jobs so they can have time with their children, or
- finding a constructive way to use the small amount of time they have with their children.[4]

Balancing the responsibilities of a job and a home has been a struggle since the Garden of Eden. In Genesis 2 God gave man a job (v. 15) and, right after that, a wife (v. 22). In the span of these short verses, Adam goes from having one major responsibility (a job) to having a second major responsibility (a home). Welcome to the real world, Adam. Here's a hoe and a wedding ring. Balancing the teeter-totter of work and the home has never been easy.

God places a high priority on the home. At a wedding, a man and a woman say vows to each other. This is not meaningless "fluff"; during the exchanging of vows, the couple is actually entering into a binding covenant with each other and with God (Prov. 2:17; Mal. 2:14). We also are told that children are an inheritance from the Lord (Psalms 127, 128). The Bible states very clearly that our families are not disposable relationships.

Most Christians know all of this, but after years of counseling, both authors can tell you that many Christians don't live by these truths. Why do we act as though our families are disposable while our jobs are not? What counsel does God give in this difficult arena? How can we win the battle of family versus work?

Let's see how the ETHICS compass can help us balance the responsibilities of work and home.

Examine the Facts

The first step in making a proper ethical decision is to make sure you have all of the facts and then examine them carefully. Why do some men and women become so obsessed with work that they slight their time and attention to their family? Why does a person become a workaholic?

A workaholic is addicted to work. *Workaholism* has been defined as a "respectable addiction." It is respectable unless you happen to be married to the workaholic. This "addiction" can be seen when the person spends more time than normal or necessary at work. How can you determine what is normal and necessary? Consider the very serious reality behind these tongue-in-cheek symptoms of workaholism:

- When you offer your children candy, they reply, "No, we're not allowed to take candy from a stranger."
- You spend more time at your email address than at your home address.
- The last time you went to your child's school for a function you got lost.
- You have so many irons in the fire that you forget what each iron is for.
- You know the company's after-hours cleaning crew by name.
- You would not dare to ask your spouse if you're a workaholic without first putting on a football helmet.

Bob knew he was becoming a workaholic, but he needed to discover why. Motivation is another way to determine whether one is a workaholic. Addiction does not just mean that you love your job. You may hate it. Addiction means that you feel you need to be there—no, you *have* to be there. You feel a compulsion to stay at work because of external or internal motivations. We use the MONEY acrostic to illustrate the five motivations for workaholics:

M—Mind-set

Some people are workaholics because they need *self-esteem*. Maybe their father never let them feel as if they measured up to his standards. A workaholic perspective also can come out of a *perfectionistic* mind-set. "No one can do the job as well as I can. Therefore, I have to be the one to do it. People need me. The company is depending on me."

We all have an inner desire to feel important. If the home does not provide for this need, often the person seeks to fill this void through spending extreme amounts of time at the office. Seeking to impress the boss is one thing, but when a person continually sacrifices other things in life to impress others, then something is wrong internally. This internal motivation will take some deep thinking or wise questioning to uncover.

O—Obligations

Bob had a job in which, if he did not put in the required, oppressive number of hours, he would be unpromotable or unemployed. Think about the absurdity of the situation. For the sake of his family, he was usually physically absent from them.

More often than not, we don't choose to spend more time at work than at home; we feel pressured to do so by our boss. Many older bosses, like Ebenezer Scrooge, are what we call "happy workaholics." Starting out, Ebenezer had a boss who was a workaholic and demanded the same of everyone else. Eventually, Ebenezer climbed the corporate ladder because of his never-quit, driving style. Ebenezer's leadership style is like the "goatherd" approach we discussed in chapter 10. Intolerant bosses like this make demands of others that are difficult to sidestep. Listen to how Charles Swindoll describes the intolerant boss:

> This person may be competent and knowledgeable, but no one can please him or her. Intolerant bosses are frequently workaholics, perfectionistic by nature, and superdemanding. The job means everything to this person. To such high-achieving, hard-charging, tough-minded skippers, enough is never enough. Unlike the incompetent leader, this person is often overqualified, demanding more than is reasonable of others. And when expectations are not met, it is the employee's fault.[5]

This type of boss is extremely difficult to work for and is usually insensitive to family issues. Thus he or she becomes the driving force in making other people work like workaholics.

N—Need

Financial need constrains many of us to spend more time away from home than we would like. Of course we need to provide for our family. First Timothy 5:8 says, "If anyone does not provide for his relatives, and especially for his immediate family, he has denied the faith and is worse than an unbeliever." But when providing becomes the driving force for spending more time at work than at home, something is wrong. It could be that the family has bought too many toys and gotten too deep into debt. Or something more insidious may have taken root in the husband's heart. The idea that the husband is to be the provider rather than the lover can spread like mold on bread. Swindoll calls this substitute for love the "enter provider . . . exit lover" approach:

> The first substitute is providing a living instead of sharing a life. One of the most common misconceptions husbands have goes something like this: "Now that I have worked hard and provided you with a nice place, sufficient food, and the clothes you need, what more could you ask of me?" But wait, husbands. Your wife married *you*, not your paycheck.[6]

Whether it is too much debt or a "provider" mentality, financial need as a motivation to be a workaholic does not provide what a family truly needs.

E—Escape

Some deliberately choose to spend more time at work than at home. For them, work provides a much-needed escape from the demands of a spouse or the stress of having to deal with the kids. At work the husband may feel like the hero, while at home he feels like a zero. At work he hears the accolades of subordinates, but at home all he hears is the nagging of a spouse or the wailing of small children. At work all the women look like babes, while at home his wife usually wears the spit-up of his babe. At work he sets the agenda, while at home he is given an agenda—a to-do list. On and on it goes, so that many choose to escape to work and after a weekend at home, their credo is "Thank God it's Monday."

Y—You

Some choose work over family because of an incessant quest to gain power, status, money, possessions, and applause. They choose themselves over everyone else, including their own families. Their careers are more important than the calling of their families.

Ascertaining which of these motivations is causing a person to overwork takes probing questions. Many times a combination of them drives a person to be a workaholic, and often even the workaholic is unaware of the driving force. If that is your situation, prayerfully evaluate your work habits on the MONEY grid. Next, because our hearts can deceive us (Jer. 17:9), we recommend that you go over the MONEY grid with your spouse and a trusted Christian friend. Bob Cratchit was on his way to becoming a workaholic by complying with the excessive demands Ebenezer Scrooge placed on his life.

(Seek the) Truth

The second step in making a proper ethical decision is to seek what God has to say about this matter. Song of Songs 2:14–15 says, "My dove in the clefts of the rock, in the hiding places on the mountainside, show me your face, let me hear your voice; for your voice is sweet, and your face is lovely. Catch for us the foxes, the little foxes that ruin the vineyards, our vineyards that are in bloom."

The "little foxes" eventually destroy the big things. All the good reasons in the world that make us workaholics are just "little foxes" that will soon destroy our marriages, "our vineyards that are in bloom." So we need to ask some important questions. What does the Bible say about the issue being faced? What does the Bible say about the MONEY grid?

M—Mind-set

The Bible has a lot to say about having proper self-esteem. What if we are driven to constantly prove ourselves and impress others at work? To be sure, we need to be excellent employers and employees (see chapter 11). But a workaholic's desire to impress the boss and others at work can become a driving passion. A good verse to remember is 2 Corinthians 10:12: "We do not dare to classify or compare ourselves with some who commend themselves. When they measure themselves by themselves and compare themselves with themselves, they are not wise." If you follow the principles laid out in this book for being an excellent employee, you will not need to compare yourself with anyone.

What does the Bible say about perfectionism? This is the concept that "no one can do the job as well as I can, so I have to be the one to do it." This is nothing but pride. Proverbs 16:18 says, "Pride goes before destruction, a haughty spirit before a fall." Proverbs 29:23 says, "A man's pride brings him low, but a man of lowly spirit gains honor." If no one else can do the job, then you haven't trained or hired people properly to take this job off your hands. Or perhaps you have not delegated other responsibilities to staff so that you have time to do the job that only you can do. Either way, you have nothing to be proud about.

O—Obligations

What about a demanding boss like Ebenezer Scrooge? How could Bob deal
with this man's approach? As we saw in chapter 11, Christian slaves are to serve
their masters and do the will of God from the heart (Eph. 6:6). Could sacrificing
family for job be the will of God? Obviously not. Also, both Ephesians 6:5 and
Colossians 3:22 classify our masters as "earthly." Their authority is secondary to
a "heavenly" master. The heavenly Master places our family above our job, and
so must we. Bob Cratchit knew that his heavenly Master and earthly master
were at odds.

N—Need

What must a godly man provide for his family (1 Tim. 5:8)? Is he to provide
money only, or should he also provide love, companionship, and time? Common
sense tells us that a godly man provides all of these things for his family. Paul
Lewis says, "Your time is the currency your children will value most. Gifts of
your presence mean more than any presents you may give. Children understand
that time is valuable; so when we have inadequate time for our children, they
eventually interpret this to mean that we don't value them."[7]

What does the Bible have to say about being overextended financially? Consider the wisdom of 1 Timothy 6:8–10, 17–19:

> But if we have food and clothing, we will be content with that. People who want
> to get rich fall into temptation and a trap and into many foolish and harmful
> desires that plunge men into ruin and destruction. For the love of money is a
> root of all kinds of evil. Some people, eager for money, have wandered from the
> faith and pierced themselves with many griefs. . . . Command those who are rich
> in this present world not to be arrogant nor to put their hope in wealth, which
> is so uncertain, but to put their hope in God, who richly provides us with every-
> thing for our enjoyment. Command them to do good, to be rich in good deeds,
> and to be generous and willing to share. In this way they will lay up treasure for
> themselves as a firm foundation for the coming age, so that they may take hold
> of the life that is truly life.

E—Escape

In Ephesians 5–6 the apostle Paul lays down some demanding requirements
for husbands and wives:

- Wives are to "submit to their husbands as to the Lord" (Eph. 5:22).
- Husbands are to "love your wives, just as Christ loved the church and gave
  himself up for her" (Eph. 5:25). "For this reason a man will leave his father

and mother and be united to his wife, and the two will become one flesh"
(v. 31).

- Fathers are to bring up their children "in the training and instruction of
the Lord" (Eph. 6:4).

Each of these requirements requires commitment and time. It is impossible
to fulfill Ephesians 5–6 from the office.

It may be easier to escape from home and go to work, but the easy thing
is not easy for long. The easy path will soon bring a world of hardship to you,
your spouse, and your kids. Running from problems, whether they be a nagging
spouse, demanding children, or rebellious teenagers, only makes matters worse
in the long run. As we saw earlier, when you were married, you and your spouse
said vows to one another and to God. It is irrelevant whether you comprehended
all the significance of what you were promising in the vows. All you need to
know is that God understood you were making vows to each other and to him.
He will hold you accountable. Listen to the somber warning from Ecclesiastes
5:4–5: "When you make a vow to God, do not delay in fulfilling it. He has no
pleasure in fools; fulfill your vow. It is better not to vow than to make a vow
and not fulfill it."

Y—You

What does the Bible say about the quest for power, money, things, or fame?
Consider the warning of Jesus: "Watch out! Be on your guard against all kinds
of greed; a man's life does not consist in the abundance of his possessions"
(Luke 12:15). The humorous saying is true: No one ever saw a hearse pulling
a U-Haul.

Ecclesiastes 4:8 lays out a particularly good description of the workaholic:
"There was a man all alone; he had neither son nor brother. There was no end to
his toil, yet his eyes were not content with his wealth. 'For whom am I toiling,'
he asked, 'and why am I depriving myself of enjoyment?' This too is meaningless—a miserable business!"

Notice the elements of the picture in Ecclesiastes. First, the man is alone
because he has been married to his job and that has resulted in estrangement
from a wife and son. Second, his work is hard ("toil") and there is no end to
it. Third, after all he has sacrificed for his wealth, he is not content. It is never
enough, and he only wants more. Fourth, he begins to understand that he won't
be able to take it with him. He has deprived himself of joy and accomplished
nothing lasting. When this man finally gets a proper perspective on wealth, it is
too late. He has sacrificed his family and is miserable and all alone. Ecclesiastes
4:8 is the workaholic's epitaph.

Hesitate

This third step in making a proper ethical decision is to see if there is anything about our decision that makes us hesitate before proceeding. What do we do when we have settled on a course of action, but we sense a "red flag" or a "little voice" whispering to us to slow down or stop altogether? Are we simply afraid to do the right thing, or is our conscience trying to tell us something?

As he worked through the steps, Bob Cratchit began to realize that he was a workaholic. He also saw that the primary reason his life was out of balance was the obligation forced on him by his boss, Ebenezer Scrooge. He then examined Bible verses that shouted at him to wake up from his foggy dream. He now knew that he needed to make changes before it was too late. He knew he needed to reconcile with his wife and Tiny Tim, and he must reorganize his work schedule.

How should he proceed? Bob needed to go to the next step for more guidance.

Identify the Greater Good

Paul Lewis recalls:

I always kissed my father goodnight and we always enjoyed a certain warmth, but we never talked seriously. We were from two different planets. He died in 1964 at age 55 when I was fourteen years old. I felt then, as I do now that he had labored tirelessly to "get ahead" at the price of never having been able to stop and try to know what it or we were all about. His was a selfless labor for kids he barely had time to know.[8]

This man shared his recollection of his workaholic father. No parent wants his or her children to remember "a selfless labor for kids he barely had time to know." The fourth step in making a proper ethical decision is to identify the greater good. The Greater Good approach holds that the priority of values places God over other persons and persons over things. When there is an unavoidable conflict between two spheres, the higher takes precedence.

Bob needed to identify the greater good and obey the higher law. As he thought this through, the greater good made his decision obvious:

- *Love for God over love for man.* Loving God is the greatest and highest commandment.
- *Love people more than things.* Bob's love for his wife and son was to be more important than his job and the things it provided.

- *Love others more than self.* Bob had to ask himself, "Am I treating my job as a treasure and my family as toys? Am I thinking more of my career than my calling as a husband and father?"
- *Obeying God rather than your boss.* Normally, the good for Bob was to obey his boss when possible. But when forced to make a choice, the greater good told Bob to obey God rather than Mr. Scrooge.

Bob knew what the overriding moral obligations were: God over your boss, people over things, and others before self. In this situation he knew what his obligations were. Now he knew *what* he should do, but *how* should he do it? That leads us to the next step.

Consider Consequences and Creative Alternatives

The fifth step in making a proper ethical decision is to consider two very important questions: What will be the consequences of your action? Are there any creative alternatives available? There's a sign along the Alaskan Highway that reads, "Choose Your Rut Carefully. You'll Be in It for the Next 200 Miles."[9] To motivate us to make the changes necessary, we need to consider the rut we are in.

What Will Be the Consequences?

Thinking through the possible consequences is a wise course of action and should not deter us from the right course of action. Rather it should prepare us for the outcome. As there is a cost to every important decision, Bob needed to prepare for it.

- If I continue to sacrifice my family for my job, what will be the short-term effects?
- What will be the long-range effects?

A man who puts his boss in front of his wife will one day be standing in front of a judge. Charles Stanley notes, "No father can bring home a paycheck large enough to buy his way out of giving time to his wife and children."[10]

- If I choose not to sacrifice my family for my job, what will be the short-term effects?
- What will be the long-range effects?
- Do I lose my job now and maybe lose my house in the future?

Have you ever really thought about what you are sacrificing for your job? Are you sacrificing time with your family to spend time with your job? Are you sacrificing your health to get ahead in your company? U.S. Bureau of Labor statistics show that the average worker in the United States works at ten or more jobs between the ages of eighteen and forty.[11] If a person has had ten jobs at age thirty-eight, how many more jobs will a person have by the age of fifty-eight? The concept of one employer for a lifetime is long gone. Why sacrifice what is most important, your family, for a transitory thing? Two things will matter over the course of your life, your family and your health. If you are sacrificing these most important things for a job, will you say on your deathbed, "I wish I'd spent more time at the office"?

Are Any Creative Alternatives Available?

When facing his ethical dilemma in the workplace, could Bob come up with a creative option to his wrong situation? To do this Bob needed to know three things:

1. What is the goal?
2. Is there a better way?
3. Is there a wise approach?

The goal. As to the goal, most bosses like Scrooge only care about the bottom line—making a profit. Knowing what the boss ultimately wants is the starting point to solving the problem.

A better way. Is there a better way to accomplish the goal? Can Bob accomplish the same results at work but still spend time with his family? This will require a whole new approach to time management. Bob can no longer be reactive to the demands on his time. For far too long he has been on a runaway stagecoach heading for a cliff. Now he must become proactive and grab the reins of time management and slow down the horses.

To move toward good time management, schedule both business meetings and family meetings in your weekly planner. As much as possible, your family meetings must be off-limits. If a client wants to meet for dinner to discuss a proposal, check your calendar. If your child has a teacher's conference that evening, simply say, "I'm sorry. I'm already booked for that evening. But we can meet. . ." Paul Lewis explains:

> Although you don't set your work schedule, because you are proactive, you use your creativity and power of choice to devise ways to spend time with your children. This could mean, of course, not taking up golf until the last child leaves for college. But you accept this as a reasonable tradeoff. The proactive dad does not beg off with the excuse, "You know I'd *like* to spend time with my children, but

with my schedule I just can't." Instead, you'll focus on the minutes you do have and make the most of them.[12]

Being proactive in your time management means you must set up some commitments. Here are some suggestions to get you started:

- *Treasure.* Work will not make me lose my family, which is my true treasure. If it gets to the point where my family is unhappy, the job goes.
- *Home.* I am home for dinner at least three nights a week and on weekends, unless traveling. If I deem it important to inform my boss when I will be late for a meeting, then I will also always inform my wife when I will be late for dinner.
- *Rest.* God rested and so must I. Weekends are for home and family, not work.
- *Presence.* Work happens at work, not at home. When I am home, I am home. If work must happen at home, it has to be either an emergency or after the kids are asleep.
- *Schedule.* I will schedule family outings and school events into my calendar just as I do a business meeting. I will block out untouchable time for my family. I will make it a point to attend recitals, plays, birthday parties, and teacher conferences.

A wise approach. If time management is the better way, what is the wise approach? How you present your position and creative alternative to your boss is very important. Just because you have adjusted your priorities does not mean your boss will agree to them. Remember that for Bob, his problem was his boss, who expected sixty- and seventy-hour work weeks. Here are some suggestions:

Look for an ally, someone in the company who is responsive to work and family needs. Maybe they have kids the same ages as yours. Discuss your family priority concerns with them. Look for a supervisor who is also balancing work and family. Get ideas from co-workers who have had experience with juggling the many roles and responsibilities that you are feeling pressured about and need to address. This isn't to get people to gang up on your boss. Rather, it is to assess the needs as well as ascertain ideas from others.

Be creative with your proposal to your boss. Keith Wells, a financial coordinator at the University of Pennsylvania, was surprised when his pregnant wife wanted him to accompany her to her weekly doctor visits. Realizing that his presence at home was important to his wife during her pregnancy, Wells decided to come up with a feasible plan for work. So he negotiated a deal with his boss to come in one hour later and leave an hour earlier to spend more time with his wife in exchange for sacrificing his lunch shift and working harder. The arrangement made his workday more hectic because Wells had less time to complete his tasks, but he said he was more energized at work and could spend extra time with his wife.[13]

Share the benefits of a family-friendly workplace. These include reduced stress levels among employees, increased loyalty and better morale, increased commitment to the job and the company, better recruiting and retention of skilled workers, and enhanced image in the community as a caring organization.

Have a plan. Let's say that you want to be able to visit your child's school or child-care site from time to time. When you approach your boss, have a plan in mind. Some employers are providing release time to allow parents to be involved in their children's programs, parent-teacher conferences, and such. Others work out comp time so parents can be involved at school. Here is a four-step example of how to approach an employer:

1. Explain why release time is a "win-win." Being allowed time off for your family is a benefit for you, but how could it also be a benefit for your boss? This is where you might share the benefits of a family-friendly environment, listed above. An excellent source of information on these benefits can be found at www.whenworkworks.org.
2. Explain how you will use the release time. For employers to support these activities, help them understand why you need this time off. Share that you need the time to attend a parent-teacher conference or a school function, such as a play or field trip.
3. Be specific in your request. If you want to be allowed to take time off to go to some of your child's school functions, then establish this understanding before the school year begins. For example, you may ask for the following:

   - two "school readiness" days a year that could be used to participate in your child's education or child-care program
   - a certain number of hours a year to increase your involvement in the schools
   - more flexibility in your schedule to visit the school/child-care site in the early morning hours or during lunch

4. Once you secure release time, keep your employer and others informed about the importance of such a benefit. If your boss gives you the time off, express your appreciation in a note or even at an employee function.

Stand for God

> When you sit to dine with a ruler,
>   note well what is before you,
> and put a knife to your throat
>   if you are given to gluttony.
> Do not crave his delicacies,
>   for that food is deceptive.
> Do not wear yourself out to get rich;
>   have the wisdom to show restraint.
> Cast but a glance at riches, and they are gone,
>   for they will surely sprout wings
>   and fly off to the sky like an eagle.
>
> Proverbs 23:1–5

This is not a new diet craze found in the Bible. Solomon here is making a symbolic statement about desiring riches. He is saying that before you covet all the riches you see, remember it is deceptive food. There are hooks in every bite. Not only that, riches are "here today and gone tomorrow." Swindoll observed that on the back of a dollar bill is a picture of an eagle with wings outstretched. That picture is accurate because the dollar bills keep flying out of our wallets.[14] Solomon's counsel is "Do not wear yourself out to get rich; have the wisdom to show restraint" (Prov. 23:4). Don't waste your time sacrificing what is most important, your family, for something that will one day just fly away.

The final step in making a proper ethical decision is to decide to stand for God no matter what. Sometimes you can get your boss to change his or her mind, as Daniel did in chapter 1. But other times this may not work, as Daniel's friends found out in Daniel 3 and Daniel himself found in chapter 6. What do you do then? To stand for God you must make two decisions:

1. *Purpose in your heart that you will stand for God no matter what.* You must choose to live for your family instead of your job.
2. *Remember that suffering leads to glory.* The Lord promises that suffering for doing right will lead to reward. He does not promise you that your boss will love you or that you will not lose your job. But God does promise that you will receive glory from him in the proper time.

Conclusion

The bottom line is this: our jobs come and go; our family is for life. We need to make wise choices with our families because we are touching eternity. Some jobs demand periods of overtime now and then. When that time has ended, you can make it up to your family with a special trip. But some bosses and companies demand that their employees sell their souls. If no amount of creative alternatives and wise approaches will work, then you must do two things—resign your job and reside in God.

Sometimes your job horror story may have a fairy-tale ending. Your boss may have a change of heart like Ebenezer Scrooge did, and he may fall in love with your child, Tiny Tim. Other times, Mr. Scrooge will always be a scrooge and saying "Humbug!" to your request for family time. Then you will know that it is time to move on to another story line.

Conclusion

Our journey began with being lost in the ethical wilderness of work. We then learned how and why we came to lose our way. We discovered the foundation for absolute values and defined what ethics looks like. The ETHICS Compass was unveiled as a practical tool to guide us when facing ethical dilemmas. We followed the ETHICS Compass through the life of Daniel as he demonstrated how to make ethical decisions in very difficult times. Finally, we applied what we have learned about ethics to some very practical areas of the workplace. These practical areas included dilemmas such as sexual challenges, and those dealing with employers, employees, and customers.

We leave you with this last example of ethics in the workplace:

> When Ted Williams was forty years old and closing out his career with the Boston Red Sox, he was suffering from a pinched nerve in his neck. "The thing was so bad," he later explained, "that I could hardly turn my head to look at the pitcher." . . . For the first time in his career he batted under .300, hitting just .254 with ten home runs. He was the highest salaried player in sports that year, making $125,000. The next year the Red Sox sent him the same contract. "When I got it, I sent it back with a note. I told them I wouldn't sign it until they gave me the full pay cut allowed. I think it was twenty-five percent. My feeling was that I was always treated fairly by the Red Sox when it came to contracts. I never had any problem with them about money. Now they were offering me a contract I didn't deserve. And I only want what I deserved." Williams cut his own salary by $31,250.[1]

Integrity never ceases to amaze others. Just try it and see!

Appendix

Business Principles from Proverbs

A compass is needed to guide people in making ethical decisions in the market-place. We have developed an ethical decision-making guide called the ETHICS Compass. The second step in this ETHICS compass is the "T" point, which stands for "truth." In making a proper ethical decision, we need to seek what God has to say about the issue being faced.

Throughout this book we have shared Bible passages to gain God's guidance in the ethical dilemma we were facing. We want to demonstrate that the Bible is not silent concerning the workplace and has great wisdom if we know where to look. One of the richest sources on ethics in the workplace is the book of Proverbs, so we end this guide with excerpts that have particular significance.

Under the business topics are related proverbs. This list can be a helpful reference for working through the ETHICS acrostic. These verses are just a starting point for your journey through work's ethical wilderness. It would be wise when you discover other passages that are helpful in ethical dilemmas to jot them down here in this chapter so you know where to find them at a moment's notice.

Advice

For lack of guidance a nation falls, but many advisers make victory sure. (11:14)

The way of a fool seems right to him, but a wise man listens to advice. (12:15)

Plans fail for lack of counsel, but with many advisers they succeed. (15:22)

Listen to advice and accept instruction, and in the end you will be wise. Many are the plans in a man's heart, but it is the LORD's purpose that prevails. (19:20–21)

Make plans by seeking advice; if you wage war, obtain guidance. (20:18)

Have I not written thirty sayings for you, sayings of counsel and knowledge, teaching you true and reliable words, so that you can give sound answers to him who sent you? (22:20–21)

Anger/Conflict

For jealousy arouses a husband's fury, and he will show no mercy when he takes revenge. (6:34)

The way of a fool seems right to him, but a wise man listens to advice. A fool shows his annoyance at once, but a prudent man overlooks an insult. (12:15–16)

A gentle answer turns away wrath, but a harsh word stirs up anger. (15:1)

A king's wrath is a messenger of death, but a wise man will appease it. (16:14)

A violent man entices his neighbor and leads him down a path that is not good. . . . Better a patient man than a warrior, a man who controls his temper than one who takes a city. (16:29, 32)

A man's wisdom gives him patience; it is to his glory to overlook an offense. A king's rage is like the roar of a lion, but his favor is like dew on the grass. (19:11–12)

It is to a man's honor to avoid strife, but every fool is quick to quarrel. (20:3)

The proud and arrogant man—"Mocker" is his name; he behaves with overweening pride. (21:24)

Do not make friends with a hot-tempered man, do not associate with one easily angered, or you may learn his ways and get yourself ensnared. (22:24–25)

Like one who seizes a dog by the ears is a passer-by who meddles in a quarrel not his own. (26:17)

Stone is heavy and sand a burden, but provocation by a fool is heavier than both. (27:3)

Mockers stir up a city, but wise men turn away anger. If a wise man goes to court with a fool, the fool rages and scoffs, and there is no peace. (29:8–9)

A fool gives vent to his anger, but a wise man keeps himself under control. (29:11)

An angry man stirs up dissension, and a hot-tempered one commits many sins. (29:22)

For as churning the milk produces butter, and as twisting the nose produces blood, so stirring up anger produces strife. (30:33)

Authority

A king delights in a wise servant, but a shameful servant incurs wrath. (14:35)

Kings take pleasure in honest lips; they value a man who speaks the truth. (16:13)

Fear the Lord and the king, my son, and do not join with the rebellious. (24:21)

A tyrannical ruler lacks judgment, but he who hates ill-gotten gain will enjoy a long life. (28:16)

Many seek an audience with a ruler, but it is from the Lord that man gets justice. (29:26)

Do not slander a servant to his master, or he will curse you, and you will pay for it. (30:10)

Deceit

The wicked man earns deceptive wages, but he who sows righteousness reaps a sure reward. (11:18)

The plans of the righteous are just, but the advice of the wicked is deceitful. (12:5)

The tongue that brings healing is a tree of life, but a deceitful tongue crushes the spirit. (15:4)

A man of perverse heart does not prosper; he whose tongue is deceitful falls into trouble. (17:20)

Food gained by fraud tastes sweet to a man, but he ends up with a mouth full of gravel. (20:17)

Do not testify against your neighbor without cause, or use your lips to deceive. (24:28)

Like a club or a sword or a sharp arrow is the man who gives false testimony against his neighbor. (25:18)

Disagreements

A perverse man stirs up dissension, and a gossip separates close friends. (16:28)

Starting a quarrel is like breaching a dam; so drop the matter before a dispute breaks out. (17:14)

It is to a man's honor to avoid strife, but every fool is quick to quarrel. (20:3)

Better to live on a corner of the roof than share a house with a quarrelsome wife. (21:9)

As a north wind brings rain, so a sly tongue brings angry looks. (25:23)

Discipline (Personal)

He who heeds discipline shows the way to life, but whoever ignores correction leads others astray. (10:17)

Whoever loves discipline loves knowledge, but he who hates correction is stupid. (12:1)

He who spares the rod hates his son, but he who loves him is careful to discipline him. (13:24)

The highway of the upright avoids evil; he who guards his way guards his life. (16:17)

He who obeys instructions guards his life, but he who is contemptuous of his ways will die. (19:16)

Dishonesty

The LORD abhors dishonest scales, but accurate weights are his delight. (11:1)

Dishonest money dwindles away, but he who gathers money little by little makes it grow. (13:11)

Food gained by fraud tastes sweet to a man, but he ends up with a mouth full of gravel. (20:17)

Do not move an ancient boundary stone set up by your forefathers. (22:28)

Envy

A heart at peace gives life to the body, but envy rots the bones. (14:30)

Do not envy wicked men. Do not desire their company. (24:1)

Do not fret because of evil men or be envious of the wicked. (24:19)

Fairness

The LORD abhors dishonest scales, but accurate weights are his delight. (11:1)

Honest scales and balances are from the LORD; all the weights in the bag are of his making. (16:11)

Differing weights and differing measures—the LORD detests them both. (20:10)

The LORD detests differing weights, and dishonest scales do not please him. (20:23)

The rich rule over the poor, and the borrower is servant to the lender. (22:7)

If you lack the means to pay, your very bed will be snatched from under you. (22:27)

Generosity/Giving

Honor the LORD with your wealth, with the firstfruits of all your crops; then your barns will be filled to overflowing, and your vats will brim over with new wine. (3:9–10)

A generous man will prosper; he who refreshes others will himself be refreshed. (11:25)

Greed

A greedy man brings trouble to his family, but he who hates bribes will live. (15:27)

He who loves pleasure will become poor; whoever loves wine and oil will never be rich. (21:17)

He who oppresses the poor to increase his wealth and he who gives gifts to the rich—both come to poverty. (22:16)

Do not wear yourself out to get rich; have the wisdom to show restraint. Cast but a glance at riches, and they are gone, for they will surely sprout wings and fly off to the sky like an eagle. (23:4–5)

If you find honey, eat just enough—too much of it, and you will vomit. (25:16)

Industriousness

Lazy hands make a man poor, but diligent hands bring wealth. (10:4)

He who works his land will have abundant food, but he who chases fantasies lacks judgment. (12:11)

From the fruit of his lips a man is filled with good things as surely as the work of his hands rewards him. (12:14)

Diligent hands will rule, but laziness ends in slave labor. (12:24)

The sluggard craves and gets nothing, but the desires of the diligent are fully satisfied. (13:4)

Dishonest money dwindles away, but he who gathers money little by little makes it grow. (13:11)

All hard work brings a profit, but mere talk leads only to poverty. (14:23)

The plans of the diligent lead to profit as surely as haste leads to poverty. (21:5)

The sluggard buries his hand in the dish; he is too lazy to bring it back to his mouth. (26:15)

Be sure you know the condition of your flocks, give careful attention to your herds. (27:23)

Four things on earth are small, yet they are extremely wise: Ants are creatures of little strength, yet they store up their food in the summer; coneys are creatures of little power, yet they make their home in the crags; locusts have no king, yet they advance together in ranks; a lizard can be caught with the hand, yet it is found in kings' palaces. (30:24–28)

Inheritance

A good man leaves an inheritance for his children's children, but a sinner's wealth is stored up for the righteous. (13:22)

A wise servant will rule over a disgraceful son, and will share the inheritance as one of the brothers. (17:2)

An inheritance quickly gained at the beginning will not be blessed at the end. (20:21)

Integrity

The man of integrity walks securely, but he who takes crooked paths will be found out. (10:9)

The integrity of the upright guides them, but the unfaithful are destroyed by their duplicity. (11:3)

Better a poor man whose walk is blameless than a fool whose lips are perverse. (19:1)

Do not move an ancient boundary stone set up by your forefathers. (22:28)

Justice

The path of the righteous is like the first gleam of dawn, shining ever brighter till the full light of day. (4:18)

The LORD abhors dishonest scales, but accurate weights are his delight. (11:1)

By justice a king gives a country stability, but one who is greedy for bribes tears it down. (29:4)

Many seek an audience with a ruler, but it is from the LORD that man gets justice. (29:26)

The righteous detest the dishonest; the wicked detest the upright. (29:27)

Laziness

The sluggard craves and gets nothing, but the desires of the diligent are fully satisfied. (13:4)

One who is slack in his work is brother to one who destroys. (18:9)

Laziness brings on deep sleep, and the shiftless man goes hungry. (19:15)

A sluggard does not plow in season; so at harvest time he looks but finds nothing. (20:4)

The sluggard's craving will be the death of him, because his hands refuse to work. (21:25)

Loans

My son, if you have put up security for your neighbor, if you have struck hands in pledge for another, if you have been trapped by what you said, ensnared by the words of your mouth, then do this, my son, to free yourself, since you have fallen into your neighbor's hands: Go and humble yourself; press your plea with your neighbor! (6:1–3)

Do not be a man who strikes hands in pledge or puts up security for debts. (22:26)

Lying

He who guards his lips guards his life, but he who speaks rashly will come to ruin. (13:3)

A truthful witness does not deceive, but a false witness pours out lies. (14:5)

Arrogant lips are unsuited to a fool—how much worse lying lips to a ruler! (17:7)

Food gained by fraud tastes sweet to a man, but he ends up with a mouth full of gravel. (20:17)

A fortune made by a lying tongue is a fleeting vapor and a deadly snare. (21:6)

He who guards his mouth and his tongue keeps himself from calamity. (21:23)

Oppressing the Poor

He who mocks the poor shows contempt for their Maker; whoever gloats over disaster will not go unpunished. (17:5)

If a man shuts his ears to the cry of the poor, he too will cry out and not be answered. (21:13)

He who oppresses the poor to increase his wealth and he who gives gifts to the rich—both come to poverty. (22:16)

Do not exploit the poor because they are poor and do not crush the needy in court. (22:22)

Poverty

Lazy hands make a man poor, but diligent hands bring wealth. (10:4)

He who despises his neighbor sins, but blessed is he who is kind to the needy. (14:21)

Better a little with the fear of the LORD than great wealth with turmoil. (15:16)

He who is kind to the poor lends to the LORD, and he will reward him for what he has done. (19:17)

He who gives to the poor will lack nothing, but he who closes his eyes to them receives many curses. (28:27)

Keep falsehood and lies far from me; give me neither poverty nor riches, but give me only my daily bread. Otherwise, I may have too much and disown you and say, "Who is the LORD?" Or I may become poor and steal, and so dishonor the name of my God. (30:8–9)

Reputation

A good name is more desirable than great riches; to be esteemed is better than silver or gold. (22:1)

What you have seen with your eyes do not bring hastily to court, for what will you do in the end if your neighbor puts you to shame? If you argue your case with a neighbor, do not betray another man's confidence, or he who hears it may shame you and you will never lose your bad reputation. (25:7–10)

Retaliation/Revenge

Do not say, "I'll pay you back for this wrong!" Wait for the LORD, and he will deliver you. The LORD detests differing weights, and dishonest scales do not please him. A man's steps are directed by the LORD. How then can anyone understand his own way? (20:22–24)

Riches

Honor the LORD with your wealth, with the firstfruits of all your crops; then your barns will be filled to overflowing, and your vats will brim over with new wine. (3:9–10)

Ill-gotten treasures are of no value, but righteousness delivers from death. (10:2)

Wealth is worthless in the day of wrath, but righteousness delivers from death. (11:4)

The house of the righteous contains great treasure, but the income of the wicked brings them trouble. (15:6)

Better a little with the fear of the LORD than great wealth with turmoil. (15:16)

How much better to get wisdom than gold, to choose understanding rather than silver! (16:16)

Better a dry crust with peace and quiet than a house full of feasting, with strife. (17:1)

An inheritance quickly gained at the beginning will not be blessed at the end. (20:21)

A fortune made by a lying tongue is a fleeting vapor and a deadly snare. (21:6)

A good name is more desirable than great riches; to be esteemed is better than silver or gold. (22:1)

Do not wear yourself out to get rich; have the wisdom to show restraint. (23:4)

By wisdom a house is built, and through understanding it is established. (24:3)

Keep falsehood and lies far from me; give me neither poverty nor riches, but give me only my daily bread. Otherwise, I may have too much and disown you and say, "Who is the LORD?" Or I may become poor and steal, and so dishonor the name of my God. (30:8–9)

Righteousness

The mouth of the righteous is a fountain of life, but violence overwhelms the mouth of the wicked. (10:11)

Whoever trusts in his riches will fall, but the righteous will thrive like a green leaf. (11:28)

In the way of righteousness there is life; along that path is immortality. (12:28)

The name of the LORD is a strong tower; the righteous run to it and are safe. (18:10)

The righteous man leads a blameless life; blessed are his children after him. (20:7)

Self-Control

A quick-tempered man does foolish things, and a crafty man is hated. (14:17)

A man's wisdom gives him patience; it is to his glory to overlook an offense. (19:11)

It is to a man's honor to avoid strife, but every fool is quick to quarrel. (20:3)

Like a city whose walls are broken down is a man who lacks self-control. (25:28)

Sexual Dilemmas

[Wisdom] will save you from the adulteress, from the wayward wife with her seductive words, who has left the partner of her youth, and ignored the covenant she made before God. For her house leads down to death, and her paths to the spirits of the dead. None who go to her return or attain the paths of life. (2:16–19)

My son, pay attention to my wisdom, listen well to my words of insight, that you may maintain discretion and your lips may preserve knowledge. For the lips of an adulteress drip honey, and her speech is smoother than oil; but in the end she is bitter as gall, sharp as a double-edged sword. Her feet go down to death; her steps lead straight to the grave. She gives no thought to the way of life; her paths are crooked, but she knows it not. (5:1–6)

Can a man scoop fire into his lap without his clothes being burned? Can a man walk on hot coals without his feet being scorched? So is he who sleeps with another man's wife; no one who touches her will go unpunished. (6:27–29)

With persuasive words she led him astray; she seduced him with her smooth talk. All at once he followed her like an ox going to the slaughter, like a deer stepping into a noose. (7:21–22)

Like a gold ring in a pig's snout is a beautiful woman who shows no discretion. (11:22)

Like a bandit she lies in wait, and multiplies the unfaithful among men. (23:28)

Speech (Ethical)

The integrity of the upright guides them, but the unfaithful are destroyed by their duplicity. (11:3)

From the fruit of his lips a man is filled with good things as surely as the work of his hands rewards him. (12:14)

Reckless words pierce like a sword, but the tongue of the wise brings healing. Truthful lips endure forever, but a lying tongue lasts only a moment. (12:18–19)

The LORD detests lying lips, but he delights in men who are truthful. (12:22)

A gentle answer turns away wrath, but a harsh word stirs up anger. (15:1)

The heart of the righteous weighs its answers, but the mouth of the wicked gushes evil. (15:28)

A wise man's heart guides his mouth, and his lips promote instruction. (16:23)

A perverse man stirs up dissension, and a gossip separates close friends. (16:28)

Even a fool is thought wise if he keeps silent, and discerning if he holds his tongue. (17:28)

He who answers before listening—that is his folly and his shame. (18:13)

The tongue has the power of life and death, and those who love it will eat its fruit. (18:21)

A gossip betrays a confidence; so avoid a man who talks too much. (20:19)

He who guards his mouth and his tongue keeps himself from calamity. (21:23)

If you argue your case with a neighbor, do not betray another man's confidence, or he who hears it may shame you and you will never lose your bad reputation. (25:9–10)

Without wood a fire goes out; without gossip a quarrel dies down. (26:20)

Stealing

The violence of the wicked will drag them away, for they refuse to do what is right. (21:7)

The accomplice of a thief is his own enemy; he is put under oath and dare not testify. (29:24)

Truthfulness

The LORD detests lying lips, but he delights in men who are truthful. (12:22)

Through love and faithfulness sin is atoned for; through the fear of the LORD a man avoids evil. (16:6)

To do what is right and just is more acceptable to the LORD than sacrifice. (21:3)

Wisdom

Trust in the LORD with all your heart and lean not on your own understanding; in all your ways acknowledge him, and he will make your paths straight. Do not be wise in your own eyes; fear the LORD and shun evil. (3:5–7)

Blessed is the man who finds wisdom, the man who gains understanding. (3:13)

Good understanding wins favor, but the way of the unfaithful is hard. (13:15)

The wise in heart are called discerning, and pleasant words promote instruction. (16:21)

Listen to advice and accept instruction, and in the end you will be wise. (19:20)

Notes

Introduction

1. Enron Corporation, *2000 Code of Ethics* (July 2000), 12, http://www.thesmokinggun.com/enron/enronethics5.html.

2. "Code of Ethics" interoffice memorandum accompanying ibid., July 1, 2000, http://www.thesmokinggun.com/enron/enronethics2.html.

3. Amey Stone, "A Post-Enron Lexicon for Wall Street," *BusinessWeek Online*, October 3, 2003, http://www.businessweek.com/bwdaily/dnflash/oct2003/nf2003103_6283_db021.htm.

Chapter 1: Marketplace Ethics—Lost in a Wilderness

1. "Honesty and Ethics Poll," The Gallup Organization, December 7, 2004, www.galluppoll.com/.

2. "Morality Meter," The Gallup Organization, March 8, 2005, www.galluppoll.com/.

3. "Confidence in Institutions," The Gallup Organization, May 22–26, 2005, www.galluppoll.com/.

4. Carter McNamara, "Complete Guide to Ethics Management: An Ethics Toolkit for Managers," Authenticity Consulting, 1999, http://www.managementhelp.org/ethics/ethxgde.htm.

5. "2006 Josephson Institute Report Card on the Ethics of American Youth: Part One—Integrity" (Summary of Data), Josephson Institute of Ethics, October 15, 2006, http://www.josephsoninstitute.org/reportcard/.

6. "Leadership: Facing Moral and Ethical Dilemmas," Center for Business and Ethics, Loyola Marymount University; reproduced by Leadership Advantage, 2001, http://leadershipadvantage.com/moralAndEthicalDilemmas.shtml.

7. John Maxwell, *There's No Such Thing as "Business" Ethics* (Nashville: Warner Faith, 2003), 11–13.

8. Joan Ryan, "A Lesson in Ethics," *San Francisco Chronicle*, November 10, 2002, D4, quoted in Maxwell, *There's No Such Thing as "Business" Ethics*, 11.

9. Ibid.

10. Frank J. Navran, "Are You Guilty of Giving Your Employees an Ethical Flea Dip?" *Leading for Results,* December 13, 2002, www.ragan.com/.

11. McNamara, "Complete Guide to Ethics Management," 4.

12. Richard McGill Murphy, "Jesus Inc.: What Does It Take to Serve God and Mammon?" *Fortune Small Business*, February 1, 2006, CNNmoney.com, http://money.cnn.com/2006/01/26/magazines/fsb/jesusinc/index.htm.

13. Maxwell, *There's No Such Thing as "Business" Ethics*, 9.

14. McNamara, "Complete Guide to Ethics Management," 5.

Chapter 2: How Did We Lose Our Way?

1. Ron Menchaca, "Lost at Sea," *The Charleston Post & Courier*, May 8, 2005, A1.

2. Frank Pellegrini, "Person of the Week," *Time*, January 18, 2002, http://www.time.com/time/pow/article/0,8599,194927,00.html.

3. Lorraine Woellart, "You Mean Cheating Is Wrong?" *Business Week*, December 9, 2002, 8.

4. Pellegrini, "Person of the Week."

5. Norman L. Geisler, *Christian Ethics: Options and Issues* (Grand Rapids: Baker, 1989), 17–22.

6. Ed Silvoso, *Anointed for Business* (Ventura, CA: Regal, 2002), 46–56.

Chapter 3: What Is Our Moral Foundation?

1. "Are Our Bridges Safe?" *Dateline*, MSNBC, May 16, 2003, http://www.msnbc.com/ (accessed November 19, 2005).

2. Norman Geisler and Randy Douglass, *Bringing Your Faith to Work* (Grand Rapids: Baker, 2005), 89–93.

3. Norman Geisler and Ron Brooks, *When Skeptics Ask* (Grand Rapids: Baker, 1990), 23.

4. See C. S. Lewis, *The Abolition of Man* (London: Oxford University Press, 1943), "Illustrations of the Tao" (appendix).

5. Gregory Koukl, "Guilt and God," *Stand to Reason* (1994), http://www.str.org/site/News2?page=NewsArticle&id=5283.

6. Norman Geisler and Frank Turek, *I Don't Have Enough Faith to Be an Atheist* (Wheaton: Crossway, 2004), 171.

7. Ibid., 172–81.

8. Ibid., 39.

9. C. S. Lewis, *Mere Christianity* (New York: Macmillan, 1952), 45.

10. Geisler and Turek, *I Don't Have Enough Faith to Be an Atheist*, 182–86.

11. "U.S. Public School Districts Overwhelmingly Promote Abstinence," Alan Guttmacher Institute, December 14, 1999, http://www.guttmacher.org/media/nr/newsrelease3106.html.

12. Lewis, *Mere Christianity*, 26.

13. J. Budziszewski, *What We Can't Not Know* (Dallas: Spence, 2003), 114.

14. Geisler, *Christian Ethics*, 135–55.

Chapter 4: What Is Ethics?

1. Terry Mayer, "Background Checks in Focus," *HR*, January 2002, http://www.findarticles.com/p/articles/mi_m3495/is_1_47/ai_82107075#continue.

2. HRM Guide, "Resume Padding," *HR*, May 31, 2002, 56, http://www.hrmguide.net/usa/recruitment/resume_padding.htm.

3. Nicole Lynch, "Bausch and Lomb CEO's Resume Falsified to Include Stern MBA," *Opportunity* 33, no. 5, November 5, 2002, http://pages.stern.nyu.edu/~opportun/issues/2002-2003/issue05/03_bausch.htm.

4. TCS Staff, "Veritas CFO Resigns Over Falsified Resume," *The Street*, October 3, 2002, http://www.thestreet.com/_tscs/markets/marketfeatures/10045724.html.

5. Erich Luening, "Lotus Stands Behind Papows," CNET *News.com*, April 30, 1999, http://news.com.com/2100-1001_3-225210.html.

6. CNN, "U.S. Olympic Chief Resigns in Resume Scandal," *CNN.com*, May 24, 2002, http://archives.cnn.com/2002/US/05/24/olympics.resignation/index.html.

7. Associated Press, "Short Tenure," *SI.com*, December 14, 2001, http://sportsillustrated.cnn.com/football/college/news/2001/12/14/oleary_notredame/.

8. Associated Press, "RadioShack CEO Resigns amid Resume Questions," *USA Today*, February 20, 2006, http://www.usatoday.com/money/industries/retail/2006-02-20-radioshack-ceo_x.htm.

9. Robin Wilson, "Fall from Grace," *The Chronicle of Higher Education* 49, no. 30, April 4, 2003, A10, http://chronicle.com/free/v49/i30/30a01001.htm.

10. William Shakespeare, *King Henry the Sixth*, pt. 3, act 5, scene 6.

11. Geisler, *Christian Ethics*, 17.

12. Geisler and Douglass, *Bringing Your Faith to Work*, 12.

13. Ibid., 31.

14. Geisler, *Christian Ethics*, 22–25.

15. J. P. Moreland and Norman L. Geisler, "Ethical Theories and Ethical Decision-Making," in *Do the Right Thing*, ed. Francis J. Beckwith (Sudbury, MA: Jones and Bartlett, 1996), 44.

16. Robin Dennison, *Pass CCRN!* (St. Louis: Mosby, 2000), 654–55.

17. Geisler, *Christian Ethics*, 25–26.

18. Ibid., 29.

19. The authors hold to the Greater Good (graded absolutism) approach.

20. Geisler, *Christian Ethics*, 116–20.

Chapter 5: The ETHICS Compass

1. These items can be viewed online at American Treasures of the Library of Congress, Memory Gallery B: Death of a President, Artifacts of Assassination, http://www.loc.gov/exhibits/treasures/trm012.html.

2. "Abraham Lincoln Papers at the Library of Congress," The Learning Page of the Library of Congress, http://memory.loc.gov/learn/collections/papers/history7.html.

3. Ibid.

4. Carl Sandburg, *Abraham Lincoln* (New York: Harcourt, Brace & World, 1954), 318.

5. Donald Phillips, *Lincoln on Leadership* (New York: Warner, 1992), 13.

6. Ibid., 21.

7. Randy Douglass shares these conflict resolution skills in his Office Zoo seminar. For more information, see his website www.workplacepeace.org.

8. Gary Smalley, *Making Love Last Forever* (Dallas: Word, 1996), 144–47.

9. Roy P. Brasler, *Collected Works of Abraham Lincoln*, vol. 7 (New Brunswick, NJ: Rutgers University Press, 1953), 542, 543.

10. David Elton Trueblood, *Abraham Lincoln: Theologian of American Anguish* (New York: Harper & Row, 1973), 96.

11. Abraham Lincoln, letter to the Voters of the Seventh Congressional District, July 31, 1846, http://showcase.netins.net/web/creative/lincoln/speeches/handbill.htm.

12. Trueblood, *Abraham Lincoln*, 73.

13. Noah Brooks, quoted in ibid.

14. Sandburg, *Abraham Lincoln*, 319.

15. Charles Sumner quoted in ibid.

16. Abraham Lincoln quoted in Sandburg, ibid., 320.

17. Ibid., 343, italics added.

18. Ibid., 314.

19. Ibid., 331.

20. Moreland and Geisler, "Ethical Theories and Ethical Decision-Making," 44.

21. Abraham Lincoln quoted in Sandburg, *Abraham Lincoln*, 315.

22. Richmond *Enquirer* quoted in Sandburg, ibid., 321.

23. Randy Douglass shares these conflict resolution skills in his Office Zoo seminar referenced in an earlier note.

24. Sandburg, *Abraham Lincoln*, 313.

25. Tertullian quoted in John MacArthur, *The MacArthur New Testament Commentary*, Matthew 1–7 (Chicago: Moody, 1985), 223.

26. Abraham Lincoln quoted in ibid., 331.

27. Ibid., 345.

Chapter 6: Between a Rock and a Hard Place

1. Renald Showers, *The Most High God* (West Collingswood, NJ: The Friends of Israel Gospel Ministry, 1982), 3–4.

2. Ibid., 5.

3. Geisler and Douglass, *Bringing Your Faith to Work*, 23–33.

4. Ibid., 19–23.

Chapter 7: Kissing Up to the Boss

1. Progressive Insurance cited in Insurance.com, "Car Accidents Tend to Occur Close to Home," Insurance.com, http://www.insurance.com/Article.aspx/Car_Accidents_Tend_to_Occur_Close_to_ Home/artid/104 (accessed October 15, 2005).

2. Lord Acton quoted in *The New Dictionary of Cultural Literacy*, 3rd ed., E. D. Hirsch Jr., Joseph F. Kett, and James Trefil (Boston: Houghton Mifflin, 2002), http://www.bartleby.com/59/13/powertendsto.html.

3. Norman Geisler and Thomas Howe, *When Critics Ask* (Grand Rapids: Baker, 1992), 294.

Chapter 8: Going with the Flow

1. Geisler and Howe, *When Critics Ask*, 294–95.

2. Showers, *The Most High God*, 60–61.

3. Warren W. Wiersbe, *The Integrity Crisis* (Nashville: Nelson, 1988), 21.

Chapter 9: Sexual Dilemmas in the Workplace

1. Susan M. Heathfield, "Women and Work: Then, Now, and Predicting the Future for Women in the Workplace," About.com, http://humanresources.about.com/od/worklifebalance/a/business_women .htm (accessed November 12, 2005).

2. Bob Sullivan, "Porn at Work Problem Persists," *MSNBC*, September 6, 2004, http://www.msnbc .msn.com/id/5899345/.

3. "Some Facts Every Employer Should Know about Sexual Harassment and What You Can Do about Them," Employers Publications, http://www.employerspublications.com/ (accessed November 17, 2005).

4. Nikki Katz, "Sexual Harassment Statistics," All Info About, http://www.allinfoaboutwomensissues. com/sexual_harassment_statistics.html (accessed November 18, 2005).

5. Lindle Beets Jr., interviewed by Randy Douglass, February 10, 2006, Mt. Pleasant, South Carolina.

6. Ibid.

7. Geisler and Douglass, *Bringing Your Faith to Work*, 25.

8. Jason Tuohey, "Office Romances Fraught with Complications," *The Boston Globe*, October 15, 2006, http://bostonworks.boston.com/news/articles/2006/10/15/office_romances_fraught_with_compli cations/?page=full.

9. Andrea C. Poe quoted in Susan M. Heathfield, "Tips about Dating, Sex and Romance at Work," About.com, http://humanresources.about.com/cs/workrelationships/a/workromance.htm (accessed November 10, 2005).

10. Rob Moll, "Workplace Romance: The New Infidelity," *Family.org* of Focus on the Family, http:// www.family.org/lifechallenges/A000000198.cfm (accessed November 10, 2005).

11. Shirley Glass, *Not "Just Friends"* (New York: Free Press, 2003), quoted in ibid.

12. David Wyrtzen, *Love without Shame* (Grand Rapids: Discovery House Publishers, 1991), 135.

13. Jerry Jenkins, *Hedges* (Brentwood, TN: Wolgemuth & Hyatt, 1989), 26.

14. Gary Smalley, *If Only He Knew* (Grand Rapids: Zondervan, 1988), 16.

15. Ibid., 71.

16. Ibid., 118.

17. Moll, "Workplace Romance."

18. Jenkins, *Hedges*, 65.

19. Wyrtzen, *Love without Shame*, 139.

20. Ibid., 142.

21. Ibid., 147.

22. Smalley, *If Only He Knew*, 100.

23. Donna L. Franklin, "When Does Flirting Become Cheating?" *Jet*, April 9, 2001, http://www.findarticles.com/p/articles/mi_m1355/is_17_99/ai_73064303.

Chapter 10: Ethical Dilemmas for Employers

1. *Wagenseller v. Scottsdale Memorial Hospital*, 147 Ariz. 370, 710 P.2d 1025 (1985), cited in John Allison and Robert Prentice, *The Legal Environment of Business*, 4th ed. (Orlando: Dryden, 1992), 513.

2. Larry Burkett, *Business by the Book* (Nashville: Nelson, 1998), 54–55.

3. Marilyn Elias, "Rudeness Poisoning U.S. Workplace," *USA Today*, June 14, 2001, http://www.usatoday.com/careers/news/2001-06-14-rudeness.htm.

4. Randy Douglass shares these conflict resolution skills in his Office Zoo seminar referenced in an earlier note.

5. Tony Horwitz, "Mr. Edens Profits from Watching His Workers' Every Move," *Wall Street Journal*, December 1, 1994, A11. The article is available online at The Pulitzer Prizes, http://www.pulitzer.org/year/1995/national-reporting/works/horwitz2.html.

6. Henry Ford quoted in Alexander Hill, *Just Business* (Downers Grove, IL: InterVarsity, 1997), 148.

7. Stephen Robbins and Mary Coulter, *Management*, 5th ed. (Upper Saddle River, NJ: Prentice Hall, 1996), 532–33.

Chapter 11: Ethical Dilemmas for Employees

1. Charles R. Swindoll, *Strengthening Your Grip* (Waco: Word Books, 1982), 206.

2. "Workplace bullying," Workplace Bully Institute, http://www.bullyinginstitute.org/bbstudies/def.html (accessed December 2, 2005).

3. John MacArthur, *Ephesians*, The New Testament Commentary (Chicago: Moody, 1986), 323.

4. Ibid.

5. Warren Wiersbe, *The Bible Exposition Commentary*, vol. 2 (Wheaton: Victor, 1989), 233.

6. "Respect" is a 1967 hit and signature song of Aretha Franklin, written and originally released by Otis Redding in 1965. Wikipedia, s.v. "Respect (song)," http://en.wikipedia.org/wiki/Respect_%28song%29 (accessed December 5, 2005).

7. Geisler and Douglass, *Bringing Your Faith to Work*, 22–24.

8. Ibid., 22–23.

9. Ibid., 23–33.

Chapter 12: Ethical Dilemmas with Customers

1. Alexander Hill, *Just Business* (Downers Grove, IL: InterVarsity, 1997), 107.

2. Peter Lavelle, "Avoiding Quacks," Health Matters of ABC.net.au, May 6, 2003, http://www.abc.net.au/health/cguides/avoidingquacks.htm.

3. Jill Homer, "Tips for Curing Bad Customer Service," PTBarticles.com, February 16, 2005, http://www.ptbarticles.com/Business/Customer-Service/11927;;Tips-for-Curing-Bad-Customer-Service.html.

4. Marilyn Adams, "Airlines Lost 10,000 Bags a Day in '05," *USA Today*, February 16, 2006, http://www.usatoday.com/money/biztravel/2006-02-16-lost-bags-usat_x.htm.

5. Art Waller quoted in Homer, "Tips for Curing Bad Customer Service."

6. Ibid.

7. Burkett, *Business by the Book*, 136–37.

8. Gary Stoller, "Companies Give Front-line Employees More Power," *USA Today*, June 26, 2005, http://www.usatoday.com/money/companies/management/2005-06-26-service-usat_x.htm.

9. Liz Pulliam Weston, "Are You a Bad Customer?" *MSN Money*, February 6, 2006, http://moneycentral.msn.com/content/Savinganddebt/consumeractionguide/P103694.asp.

10. Joshua Freed, "The Customer Is Always Right? Not Anymore," *San Francisco Chronicle*, July 5, 2004, http://www.sfgate.com/.

11. "Advertising Guidelines," Neal & McDevitt (attorneys at law), 2003, http://www.nealmcdevitt.com/articles/advertisingguidelines.pdf at http://www.nealmcdevitt.com/.

12. "Truth in Advertising," *gizmag*, June 2, 2005, http://www.gizmag.com/go/4097/.

13. Quoted in Robert Alden, *Proverbs* (Grand Rapids: Baker, 1983), 150.

14. Pat Quinn quoted in Suzanne Le Mignot, "New Legislation Would Prevent Overpricing," *CBS2 Chicago.com*, February 4, 2006, http://cbs2chicago.com/local/local_story_035165905.html.

Chapter 13: Ethical Dilemmas with Balancing Work and the Home

1. Gary Kiger and Pam Riley, "Helping Dual-Earner Couples Balance Work and Family Responsibilities," Utah State University, April 2000, CYFERnet, http://www.cyfernet.org/parent/workandfamily/utah_findings.html.

2. "Poll: Women Strive to Find Balance," *CBS News*, May 14, 2006, http://www.cbsnews.com/stories/2006/05/14/opinion/polls/main1616577.shtml.

3. David Lewis quoted in Tim Simmers, "Workaholic Obsession Takes Toll," *Oakland* (CA) *Tribune*, December 9, 2005, http://www.findarticles.com/p/articles/mi_qn4176/is_20051210/ai_n15920862.

4. Paul Lewis, *The 5ive Key Habits of Smart Dads* (Grand Rapids: Zondervan, 1994, 16).

5. Charles Swindoll, *Living on the Ragged Edge* (Waco, TX: Word, 1985), 220.

6. Charles Swindoll, *Strike the Original Match* (Portland, OR: Multnomah, 1980), 61–62.

7. Lewis, *The 5ive Key Habits of Smart Dads*, 140.

8. Ibid., 137.

9. Swindoll, *Living on the Ragged Edge*, 314.

10. Charles Stanley, *A Man's Touch* (Wheaton: Victor, 1977), 39.

11. " Number of Jobs Held, Labor Market Activity, and Earnings Growth Among the Youngest Baby Boomers: Results From a Longitudinal Survey Summary," U.S. Bureau of Labor Statistics, March 11, 2005, http://www.bls.gov/news.release/nlsoy.nr0.htm (news release dated August 25, 2006).

12. Lewis, *The 5ive Key Habits of Smart Dads*, 84–85.

13. Keith Wells quoted in Tatsha Robertson, "Between Work and Life There's Balance," *The Boston Globe*, June 19, 2005, E1, http://www.mwfam.com/frameset.html.

14. Swindoll, *Living on the Ragged Edge*, 168.

Conclusion

1. Story as told by Charles Swindoll, *The Tale of the Tardy Oxcart* (Nashville: Word, 1998), 306–7.

Norman L. Geisler is the dean of Southern Evangelical Seminary and Bible College and one of the world's leading Christian apologists. He has produced over seventy books and defended the cause of Christ throughout the United States and abroad for over fifty years. For more information about Dr. Geisler or Southern Evangelical Seminary and Bible College, visit the websites www.normgeisler.com or www.ses.edu.

Randy Douglass is the founder and chairman of Workplace PEACE (Workplace Professionals for Ethics, Advocacy, and Conflict Education). This is a network of professionals dedicated to ethical decision-making and harmony in the workplace. Dr. Douglass is also the founder and president of Office Zoo Solutions, a business specializing in conflict resolution and employee motivation. He has served as a pastor, seminary professor, business executive, and consultant. For more information about these organizations or to have Dr. Douglass speak at your business, organization, or church, visit the website www.workplacepeace.org.

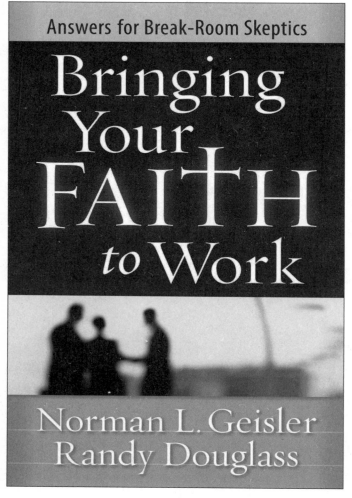